Generis
PUBLISHING

Live in the Opportunity Zone

SALIMA: An Innovative Model of Transformative Leadership

Yossi Sharabi

Title: **Live in the Opportunity Zone**

SALIMA: An Innovative Model of Transformative Leadership

ISBN: 979-8-89248-575-3

Author: Yossi Sharabi

Cover image: www.pixabay.com

Publisher: Generis Publishing
Online orders: www.generis-publishing.com
Contact email: info@generis-publishing.com

Table of Contents

Overture

This book encompasses a rich blend of theoretical and educational materials, but its true uniqueness lies in its narrative—the story of my managerial life. The numerous insights presented here stem from substantial managerial experiences that have profoundly impacted the lives of many citizens in Jerusalem and across the State of Israel. These experiences form the core of this management journey.

Over several decades, I have engaged in significant administrative roles, ranging from neighborhood management to overseeing the city's leisure systems, leading the Ministry of Culture and Sports in the Israeli government, and ultimately managing the most prominent sports organization in the country—the Israel Football Association. Each role presented me with a wealth of experience and unique managerial challenges. What makes my experience distinctive is that every organization I joined was in a state of organizational crisis, necessitating change, renewal, and growth.

My success in my initial role as the manager of the Gonenim neighborhood in Jerusalem led to repeated requests to serve as CEO of various crisis-stricken organizations. This pattern continued in managing the Pisgat Ze'ev neighborhood and the leisure systems within the municipality. Over time, I developed a reputation for managing crises effectively. I vividly recall that upon completing my tenure at the city and moving on to lead the Ministry of Culture and Sports in the Government of Israel, I received a shirt with the words: "If you recognize a crisis, turn to Yossi—he is the one to handle it."

Throughout my career, I have continually explored and documented my insights. What drives successful change? What is essential for achieving it? How do you engage employees? How do you recruit partners? Is there a winning formula? Are these traits inherent or developed over time?

This book is the culmination of my doctoral thesis and the model I developed for transformational leadership and change management. However, it is also a reflection of a rich tapestry of experiences and insights, interwoven with theoretical frameworks, that gave birth to the "Living in the Opportunity Zone" model, known as SALIMA: An Innovative Model of Transformative Leadership.

This book is about leadership that fosters change. It is intended for anyone interested in delving into leadership challenges and acquiring practical tools for leading transformations. It targets managers in various positions but also extends its reach to individuals in the broader community, even those who do not occupy formal management roles. Readers will discover that leadership is a behavior not confined by formal status; everyone can—and should—be a leader, capable of influencing and instigating change, each driven by their motivations.

I am deeply grateful to the many remarkable individuals who have accompanied me along this extensive administrative journey. I have learned from each of them. I am profoundly thankful to my parents, Meir and Shula, who have been a constant source of inspiration. My mother, Shula Sharabi, was the first transformative leader I encountered—a woman with an extraordinary ability to impact people, armed with immense empathy, infectious optimism, mental strength, and a simple yet profound personal vision: to bring joy through her remarkable culinary creations. With her magic touch, she enchanted everyone around her. She was a human magnet, drawing in people who sought strength, energy, optimism, guidance, and direction. Among her visitors were world leaders, ministers, ambassadors, and media personalities who frequented her chef's restaurant, "Reputation." Often, I felt that her exceptional food was merely an excuse for people to meet her, to unburden themselves, and to draw from her well of faith and confidence.

I am grateful to all my teachers, whether in the Faculty of Law, the School of Business Administration, or the countless workshops and seminars that enriched my understanding of leadership and transformation. Special acknowledgment is due to the two programs I participated in: the Wexner Foundation program at the Kennedy School at Harvard and the Landmark program. Both deepened my comprehension of transformative processes. I am also indebted to the thousands of employees I have met as a manager and colleague; observing them has taught me invaluable lessons. I express my gratitude to my mentors, particularly Ranan Dinor, who inspired me during his tenure as CEO of the Jerusalem Municipality.

Finally, I owe a debt of gratitude to my beloved children, Keren, Lior, and Shahar, who have been, and continue to be, my source of energy, inspiration, and the driving force behind my endeavors. To my partner, Yafit Sherer, I extend my heartfelt thanks for being my anchor and unwavering support, especially when managing daily crises.

Chapter 1: Leadership

1.1 The Development of Leadership Research

The study of leadership has profoundly evolved throughout the 20th century, marked by shifting paradigms and changing perspectives. The earliest approach to understanding leadership, the Trait Approach, dominated from the early 1900s to the late 1940s. This approach was founded on the hypothesis that leaders inherently differ from others due to specific traits they are born with. It viewed leadership as a collection of extraordinary characteristics that distinguished specific individuals as natural leaders.

However, as more research emerged, it became apparent that this trait-based perspective had significant limitations. A comprehensive review of the literature showed a need for consistent patterns in the traits associated with leadership. Studies often needed to replicate findings, and the traits identified in one context only reliably appeared in others (Shala et al., 2021). By 1948, researchers concluded that a fixed set of traits could not adequately explain leadership; instead, a leader's effectiveness depended highly on the context in which they operated (Stogdill, 1948).

In the 1950s, leadership research shifted from traits to behaviors, particularly toward understanding which styles were most effective in achieving organizational goals. This led to the study of Leadership Styles, emphasizing mission-oriented versus people-oriented approaches. While some studies suggested a positive relationship between a considerate leadership style and employee satisfaction, the findings were often inconsistent and did not persist across different situations (Bass, 1985). Although this behavioral approach contributed significantly to our understanding of leadership, it could not definitively link specific styles to effectiveness.

Over the past few decades, research on leadership has shifted dramatically from focusing solely on the individual leader to exploring a broader range of variables and their interactions. This evolution in leadership studies moved beyond personal trait analysis to investigate styles, behaviors, situations, and other factors. The concept of Leadership Style gained prominence, emphasizing a leader's tendency to adopt specific actions or behaviors in particular situations (Fuller, 2021).

Behavioral and contingent approaches have produced various models to examine organizational leadership styles from multiple perspectives. For example, Lewin, Lippitt, and White (2021) developed the Democratic-Autocratic Leadership Model, identifying three primary leadership styles—autocratic, democratic, and laissez-faire—and investigated their impacts on organizational productivity and satisfaction (Fuller, 2021).

Significant contributions to leadership theory came from the Michigan and Ohio schools, which offered two theoretical principles expressed through behavioral dimensions:

1. **Task Orientation**: The Michigan research described this as "task-oriented" leadership, while the Ohio approach referred to it as "structure-initiating" (Popper, 2007; 2015, Oplatka).
2. **People Orientation**: Michigan researchers termed this "employee-oriented" leadership, while the Ohio approach called it "consideration" (Fuller, 2021).

Although these approaches share similarities, there are notable differences. The Michigan research viewed leadership style as a one-dimensional variable ranging from task-oriented to employee-oriented (Li, Castano, & Li, 2018). In contrast, the Ohio School treated these dimensions as independent, allowing managers to be ranked high or low in either behavior.

This framework led to models such as Blake and Mouton's Managerial Grid, which identified five central leadership styles based on task and people orientations (Li et al., 2018). The Likert Scale (in Li et al., 2018) integrated findings from Michigan research, while Bowers and Seashore (Fuller, 2021) offered a theory explaining leadership effectiveness by combining insights from Michigan and Ohio studies. These contributions highlighted the need to study the behaviors of both leaders and followers.

1.2 The Situational Approach and Leadership Effectiveness

The Situational Approach further advanced the field of leadership studies by adding a situational dimension to the two primary orientations, suggesting that leadership effectiveness depends on the context. Fiedler's model, for instance, examined leadership styles as a one-dimensional variable—either task- or consideration-oriented—across nine possible situations to determine the most effective style in each (Popper, 2007). Similarly, Reddin's Three-Dimensional Model added a third dimension to assess group effectiveness alongside task- and people orientations (Popper, 2007). The Life-Cycle Model by Hersey and Blanchard (2015, Oplatka) introduced the "follower maturity" dimension, proposing that leadership effectiveness is contingent upon group development.

Additional situational models, such as Yukl's determinants of leadership effectiveness (1971) and the Path-Goal Model (House & Mitchell, in Fuller, 2022), explored how leadership styles impact followers' motivation and satisfaction. These models underscored the dynamic relationship between leadership styles, situational variables, and organizational effectiveness.

1.3 Transformational Leadership and the Paradigm Shift

Initially developed within political science (Popper, 2007), transformational leadership theory marked a paradigm shift in organizational leadership research. Bass (1985) applied this approach to organizations, distinguishing between two central styles: transactional, based on exchange relationships and rewards, and transformational, which are considered more effective in advanced organizations (Li et al., 2018). Transactional leadership is viewed as adequate but limited, while transformational leadership is more beneficial, fostering intrinsic motivation and commitment beyond external rewards (2017, Arar).

Leadership is defined as a non-aggressive influence exerted by an individual on individual and collective activities (Popper, 1999). Numerous behaviors constitute leadership, each varying in its impact on followers. The Full Range Leadership Model (Bass & Avolio, 1994) categorizes leadership behaviors into three patterns: transformational, transactional, and laissez-faire (non-leadership).

1.4 The Contingency Approach and Modern Leadership Research

In the 1960s, the contingency approach added a situational dimension to leadership research, positing that situational factors influence the effectiveness of a leader's behavior. Researchers adhering to this approach examined group tasks, environmental conditions, and follower characteristics (Bass & Avolio, 1994). However, this perspective viewed leaders primarily as reactors to situations rather than initiators or transformers (Popper, 2007).

By the 1970s, leadership research had declined significantly due to inconsistencies and contradictions in the findings accumulated over decades. However, a resurgence occurred in the late 1970s, with new theoretical developments shifting the focus back to the leader-follower relationship as a critical factor in understanding leadership behavior and effectiveness (Bass, 1985).

1.5 Defining Leadership: Beyond Management

Many definitions of leadership converge on the leader's capacity for strategic decision-making and vision, persuading others to follow and act accordingly. A common thread is the ability of leaders to create a vision and inspire others to strive toward it, motivating them with an infectious drive to achieve success (Bass & Avolio, 1994).

While leadership and management are often used interchangeably, they are distinct. Both managers and leaders manage resources, but leadership involves more, such as inspiring followers. A leader must inspire the entire organization (Bass, 1985).

Influential leaders adhere to a shared vision aligned with core values, understanding what their teams need to achieve their goals. They inspire, direct, and support their staff creatively and confidently, fostering passion, responsibility, and independence to achieve long-term success (201 ,אופלטקה8).

Leadership also involves building and organizing teams, setting goals, developing strategies, and leading employees through processes, often through personal engagement (Bass & Avolio, 1994). Leaders create valuable goals that inspire followers to strive for a shared vision beyond their immediate responsibilities (El-Sayed & El-Sayed, 2019).

1.6 Transformational Leadership and its Impact

Burns (1978) introduced transformational leadership, differentiating between transactional and transformational styles. Transactional leadership is based on precise demands and rewards, while transformational leadership encourages change, development, and empowerment, motivating followers to exceed expectations (Hater & Bass, 1988). Studies have found positive relationships between transformational leadership and follower satisfaction, motivation, commitment, and performance (El-Sayed & El-Sayed, 2019; Fayed, Fathy, 2022).

Popper et al. (2007) proposed a framework for understanding leader development, suggesting that leadership derives from potential, motivation, and a growth process. To become a prominent leader, one must possess psychological capabilities, a solid drive to lead, and developmental opportunities, such as positive experiences and influential role models (Avolio et al., 1999).

The current research is based on an innovative, transformative leadership model that uniquely focuses on the psychological characteristics necessary for leadership.

1.7 Distinctions in Leader Characteristics

Two significant distinctions elucidate leader characteristics: "personal-negative" leaders, who are narcissistic and seek constant praise, and "social-positive" leaders, who aim to contribute morally to their communities (El-Sayed & El-Sayed, 2019; Breevaart & Zacher, 2019). Additionally, leaders can be "distant," impacting followers through symbolic means, or "close," influencing through direct, everyday behaviors (Popper, 2012; Fayed, Fathy, 2022).

1.8 Leaders' Psychological Characteristics

Recently, there has been a renewed focus on the personality traits of leaders, revisiting questions posed during the era of the trait-based approach. The difference now lies in the empirical, reliable, and valid measurement tools employed in current research, which are grounded in new psychological concepts (Poetz & Volmer, 2024).

Most research in this area utilizes the Big Five model (Tao et al., 2022), a popular and reliable framework for studying personality. A meta-analysis of this model (Judge et al., 2002) identified four elements closely associated with leadership: extraversion, conscientiousness, openness to experience, and low neuroticism. These findings are consistent with earlier studies on leaders' personality traits (Bass, 1990). Personality variables, such as optimism and locus of control, have also been frequently linked to leadership in various studies (Garzon-Lasso et al., 2023). However, this body of literature questions how unique these traits are to leaders versus non-leaders.

To address this, Popper et al. (2004) conducted field research within the Israeli Defense Forces involving 402 soldiers who had recently completed basic training. The study compared perceived leadership qualities between "leaders" (those perceived as leaders by their peers or commanders) and "non-leaders." It examined several key traits identified in leadership literature, including trait anxiety, self-efficacy, optimism, locus of control, and openness to experience. The research found significant differences between the two groups: "Leaders" exhibited lower levels of trait anxiety and higher levels of self-efficacy, optimism, internal locus of control, and openness to experience compared to "non-leaders." Based on these findings, Popper and Amit (2009) argued that the core psychological traits of influential social and close leaders could be grouped into four categories: self-confidence, future orientation, initiative, and openness to experience.

1.9 Key Psychological Traits in Leadership

1.9.1 Self-Confidence

Self-confidence is critical to a leader's effectiveness (Bass, 1985; Judge et al., 2002). Research examining followers' perspectives supports this view. For example, Smith and Foti (1998) found that the most influential leadership trait perceived by followers was the self-confidence attributed to their leader. The most measurable indicators of self-confidence are low trait anxiety and high general self-efficacy (Popper & Amit, 2009).

1.9.2 Trait Anxiety

The literature distinguishes between state anxiety, a temporary emotional response to stressful situations, and trait anxiety, a personality characteristic that manifests across various situations (Spielberger, 1972). Individuals with higher levels of trait anxiety often struggle to function effectively when exposed to stress or uncertainty. Leaders typically exhibit low levels of trait anxiety, allowing them to remain calm and effective in transformative and stressful circumstances, thereby providing stability and confidence to their followers. Popper et al.'s study (2004) identified trait anxiety as the most distinguishing factor between leaders and non-leaders, aligning with findings that show a significant negative correlation between leadership and neuroticism in the Big Five model (Judge et al., 2002).

1.9.3 Self-Efficacy

Developed by Bandura (1977), self-efficacy is defined as an individual's belief in their ability to execute the actions required to achieve specific goals successfully. This perception develops gradually through a learning process where an individual accumulates experiences of success, reinforcing their sense of competence. Initially, self-efficacy was defined in the context of specific tasks. Still, the concept has since expanded to encompass a general, stable trait reflecting a person's overall confidence in their ability to perform various functions in various situations. Research supports a positive relationship between self-efficacy and leadership; leaders must believe in their capacity to manage diverse tasks and challenges, both present and future. Popper et al. (2004) found that leaders demonstrated significantly higher self-efficacy than non-leaders.

Self-efficacy influences motivation by guiding an individual's actions toward anticipated goals. People who believe in their capabilities set goals, plan activities, and persist in their efforts to achieve desired outcomes (Bandura, 1977). Individuals' perception of their abilities evolves, shaped by cumulative experiences and feedback. For instance, a person may develop confidence in mathematical skills through repeated successes and positive reinforcement. Thus, self-efficacy is a function of innate talent and a product of cognitive processes that form over time (Popper et al., 2004).

1.9.4 Future Orientation

A trait consistently attributed to leaders is their ability to forge new paths by conveying inspiring and energizing messages. To maintain a future orientation—formulating it as a compelling vision, believing in its promise of success, and persuading others to follow this direction—a leader must possess optimism (Xu et al., 2022).

Leaders with a long-term future orientation understand the value of delaying immediate gratification to achieve long-term rewards. They prioritize investment, saving, and making present sacrifices to enhance future opportunities and reach their goals (Rick, 2018).

Future-oriented individuals typically hold a positive outlook and a strong belief in their ability to shape their future. Such leaders demonstrate resilience in the face of setbacks, learning from these experiences while maintaining their motivation to strive consistently toward long-term objectives. Additionally, future-oriented leaders are often called upon to advance into new roles and exhibit greater global awareness, cultural sensitivity, a focus on sustainability, and a commitment to justice, extending their influence beyond their immediate leadership roles (Xu et al., 2022).

1.9.5 Optimism

Optimism is an individual's tendency to believe that their overall life experiences will result in more positive than adverse outcomes. It is a stable personal trait, existing beyond specific times and places, and is not constrained by any particular framework (Monehin & Diers-Lawson, 2022). Numerous studies have found a positive relationship between optimism and leadership. For instance, a comparative study examining leadership versus non-leadership traits among Israeli Defense Army commanders found that leaders were significantly more optimistic than non-leaders (Popper et al., 2004). Additionally, these studies revealed that optimism is a strong predictor of other critical leadership traits, such as the ability to present an inspiring vision for the future and the determination to achieve it (Techo & Vincent, 2021).

1.9.6 Initiative

The very essence of leadership involves taking the initiative, driving improvement, and transforming ideas into actions. The locus of control is one personality variable that closely mirrors this initiative aspect. Today, organizational leaders must exercise less direct control and instead rely on adaptive thinking to apply their skills effectively in dynamic environments (Manolika, 2023).

1.9.7 Locus of Control

First defined by Rotter (1966), locus of control refers to an individual's perceived ability or inability to influence events. Individuals with an intrinsic locus of control believe they have the personal capability to affect outcomes; therefore, they see the results of their behavior as dependent on their skills and abilities. Conversely, individuals with an extrinsic locus of control believe that external factors dictate events, meaning the outcomes of their behavior depend on other people and the difficulty level of the tasks they face. Rather than being a fixed personal trait, locus of control is considered a situational variable.

Research on locus of control within transformational and transactional leadership has shown a significant positive relationship between transformational leadership and a high intrinsic locus of control. Howell and Avolio (1993) found that transformational leaders are likelier to possess a high inherent locus of control than non-leaders.

1.9.8 Openness to Experience

Openness to Experience is one of the factors in the Big Five model of personality. This factor assesses an individual's tendency to actively seek out new experiences and their level of psychological complexity. A high score in this dimension indicates a solid inclination to pursue new experiences for their own sake. It is associated with reflectiveness, curiosity, intellectualism, imagination, creativity, and the ability to focus attention across various domains. This personality trait is stable over time (Manolika, 2023).

As mentioned earlier, a significant positive relationship exists between openness to experience and leadership (Judge et al., 2002). This finding aligns with the emphasis in social leadership literature on the importance of traits like resilience, flexibility, intellectual openness, and creativity (Bass, 1985). Such characteristics enable leaders to stimulate intellectual curiosity in their followers, encouraging them to ask questions, challenge traditional thinking methods, and explore new approaches. Intellectual stimulation is one of the four components of the Full Range Leadership Model in transformational leadership (Bass & Avolio, 1994).

Furthermore, openness to experience is considered a positive factor in leadership development. The underlying hypothesis is that leaders willing to reflect on themselves and their environment without rigid self-defense honestly will be more open to learning opportunities through observations, experiences, or learning from others (Popper & Amit, 2009). Research by Popper et al. (2004) supports this hypothesis, showing that leaders have significantly higher levels of openness to experience than non-leaders.

Chapter 2: Transformational Leadership

2.1 Background

In recent decades, extensive research has established transformational leadership as the most effective style for achieving organizational success, often outperforming other leadership styles. Transformational leadership profoundly impacts followers by inspiring them to achieve goals beyond their initial expectations. This style emphasizes the leader's role as both an emotional and behavioral catalyst who instills in followers a belief in their capacity for moral and social development (Teho & Vincent, 2021).

The outcomes of transformational leadership have been studied from various perspectives. Both psychologically and organizationally, transformational leaders—those perceived as such by their followers—are seen as capable of fostering a sense of autonomy, enhancing capabilities, strengthening organizational belonging, and clarifying a vision for their followers. In contrast, leaders perceived as transactional, who base their leadership on exchange relationships, are often associated with increased burnout and decreased motivation among followers (Popper, 2007).

The Full Range Leadership Model (Bass, 1985; Bass & Avolio, 1994) distinguishes three types of leadership: transformational, transactional, and laissez-faire. Transformational leadership comprises four key behaviors: inspiring motivation, intellectual stimulation, individualized consideration, and idealized influence (role modeling). Over the past three decades, research has highlighted the many advantages of transformational leadership, particularly its adaptability and effectiveness across diverse settings (Bass & Avolio, 1994).

Transformational leadership involves influencing others by paying attention to their needs, listening, and motivating them to make decisions that drive significant change in people and organizations (Buil et al., 2019). While often discussed in organizational contexts, transformational leadership is highly relevant in critical thinking. Transformational leaders help individuals realize their potential by enabling them to achieve their goals in beneficial and rewarding ways for themselves, their peers, and their communities (Bass & Riggio, 2006).

Research suggests that transformational leadership is associated with supporting employee autonomy and fostering a sense of trust and authenticity. The perceived authenticity and trust that employees feel toward their manager can predict the presence of transformational leadership behaviors (Teho & Vincent, 2021). In contrast, transactional leadership, which is less adaptive on the continuum of leadership styles, is based on "give-and-take" relationships between leaders and followers. This style involves using rewards and punishments to motivate followers to meet expected standards and facilitate the exchange of information and activities. Since this approach primarily relies on external motivation, followers of transactional leaders are likely to meet only the minimum required expectations without exceeding them (אופלטקה, 2018).

Influential transformational leaders are often seen as charismatic, trustworthy, and inspiring. The trait of idealized influence enables team members to view the leader as a role model—someone who demonstrates exemplary behavior and sets a standard worth following. This idealized influence allows transformational leaders to create a shared vision, inspire team members to strive toward that vision, and ultimately lead to improved performance, increased engagement, and higher job satisfaction (Bass & Riggio, 2006).

Transformational leaders recognize that every employee is unique, with distinct skills and the ability to contribute to the organization. They must ensure individualized attention and consideration for each team member, demonstrating genuine care for their well-being and growth. By practicing individualized consideration, transformational leaders take the time to understand their employees' strengths, weaknesses, and needs, providing personalized support, feedback, and training to help employees fully realize their potential (Teho & Vincent, 2021).

2.2 Transformational Leadership in Light of the Full Range of Leadership Model

Transformational leadership is characterized by a higher position on the two-dimensional spectrum of activity and affectivity and is considered an adaptive type of leadership. Bass (1997) defines a transformational leader as someone who encourages followers to perform at levels beyond their initial expectations and align their personal goals with the organizational objectives. Bass identifies four specific behaviors that collectively define transformational leadership:

- **Motivating by Inspiration**: This behavior focuses on a leader's vision, reflecting a well-integrated sense of self-identity. Leaders who employ this style encourage followers to align with their ideas by promoting a clearly defined, attractive, and relevant vision. These leaders often emphasize investing in the present to achieve a better future.
- **Serving as a Role Model**: Transformational leaders lead morally and behaviorally by example, inspiring followers to emulate their strategies and

actions. A leader's willingness to sacrifice personal interests for organizational goals demonstrates strength in those goals (Popper, 2007).

- **Intellectual Stimulation**: Transformational leaders encourage followers to face challenges and express confidence in their abilities. They challenge existing norms and problem-solving strategies, empowering followers to develop independent problem-solving skills. As a result, followers are more likely to engage in deeper, independent, and critical thinking and find innovative ways to perform tasks, taking greater responsibility for solutions.
- **Individualized Consideration**: This behavior involves developing personal relationships with followers and demonstrating genuine concern for their professional and personal development. Leaders express this relationship through mentoring and support, fostering connection and reassurance in their followers' belief in the organization. Leaders who practice individualized consideration are perceived as caring and attentive, which can reduce frustration and competition among followers and enhance their willingness to cooperate. Such leaders strive to create strong team relationships and show a caring and understanding approach.

In recent decades, these transformational leadership characteristics have significantly affected various aspects of organizational effectiveness. Research has demonstrated that transformational leadership predicts organizational commitment, reflecting an emotional and identification-based connection with the organization and influencing managers' decisions about maintaining or leaving their positions (Crede et al., 2019). Other studies suggest that transformational leaders encourage followers to apply their interpretations to organizational goals by demonstrating behaviors aligned with a clear and idealistic organizational vision. This approach enables followers to derive meaning from their work and the organization's broader objectives. As identification with goals is a crucial aspect of autonomous motivation, transformational leadership can foster such motivation among followers (Jiang & Chen, 2018).

The adaptive nature of transformational leadership can be applied to all leaders, as it requires them to possess a deep understanding of the transformational process and the ability to identify and respond to their team's needs. This often involves proactively managing resistance to change and establishing a culture of trust and collaboration within the organization. In this way, the traditional top-down authority model is replaced by a leader who functions more as a mentor than an authoritarian figure.

2.3 Strategic Transformational Leadership

Transformational leadership fosters a learning environment that empowers followers to unite around a common goal, enabling organizations to become more responsive to changes in their external environment. Managers increasingly recognize the wealth of information on how transformational leadership strategies are linked to productivity, profitability, and competitive advantage. For example, intellectual stimulation, an essential aspect of transformational leadership, can enhance leadership effectiveness by fostering a culture of learning, knowledge sharing, and collaboration (Jiang & Chen, 2018).

The transformational leadership strategy suggests that managers can inspire their teams by adapting transformative leadership techniques. By employing these strategies, managers can effectively address the critical questions surrounding management application and avoid the trial-and-error approach of uncertain leadership strategies (Buil et al., 2019).

Transformational leaders are defined by their vision and ability to develop a shared, inspiring vision for the future. They play a crucial role in transforming organizations to innovate new services and products, responding dynamically to market demands by raising expectations, exploring new opportunities, and developing strategies to meet the needs of the organization, its employees, and clients (Jiang & Chen, 2018).

One qualitative study examined how university leaders used transformational leadership strategies to adapt their institutions' operations during and after the COVID-19 pandemic. Based on Bass's (1985) Transformational Leadership Model, the guiding research question was: "What transformative leadership strategies did university leaders choose to change their university environments?" Using a narrative research approach, the study collected and analyzed publicly available data, identifying four key themes of transformational leadership practices: idealized influence, inspirational motivation, intellectual stimulation, and individualized consideration.

The findings revealed that transformational leaders exhibit high moral standards, personal charisma, and a solid commitment to influencing others while fostering a culture of growth, progressive thinking, and excellence. They encourage creative exploration, critical thinking, and collaborative, "out-of-the-box" approaches. Additionally, they cultivate personal connections, acknowledge and validate emotions, and take an individual approach, allowing employees to express their concerns. This research contributes to understanding transformational leadership in higher education, providing university leaders with insights on how to lead their teams more effectively in a rapidly changing global economy (Hardman, 2023).

Bass's Transformational Leadership Theory (1985) is a seminal framework that has enriched the field by providing methods for evaluating and scaling transformational leadership and encouraging leaders to use more authentic and focused energy to inspire their team members to emulate their values and behaviors. According to Bass, transformational leaders inspire trust, admiration, loyalty, and respect among followers.

By fostering these feelings, transformational leaders create a work environment where followers are motivated to exceed their initial expectations and work harder than they thought possible. This approach goes beyond self-interest, offering followers an inspiring mission and a sense of self-identity.

Bass's Transformational Leadership Theory (1985) excites followers by fostering inspiration and commitment to the organizational vision, nurturing innovation, and supporting follower development through training and support. The model demonstrates how transformational leadership can enhance creativity, manage crises, implement change, and develop leaders. It emphasizes idealized influence, where leaders serve as role models and set standards for others.

2.4 Transformational Leadership and Adaptation

Adaptive leaders focus on developing their skills and those of their team members, particularly in areas crucial for managing change, such as problem-solving, decision-making, and emotional intelligence. They aim to foster an environment that encourages team members to contribute their genuine viewpoints rather than relying solely on external opinions and insights for motivation.

Adaptive leaders understand the challenges of transformational change and strive to create a collaborative environment that embraces change. This approach involves cultivating a supportive atmosphere centered on relationship development, trust-building, and mutual understanding among team members. Moreover, they prioritize communication by actively seeking team feedback (Barthel & Hess, 2020).

Transformational leadership, like adaptive leadership, emphasizes inspiration and motivation to maximize the potential of individuals. Both leadership styles seek to create an environment where employees feel empowered and take ownership of their roles, driving them to achieve their goals (Heifetz & Linsky, 2017).

The fundamental principles of transformational leadership include setting a vision, providing support, and offering clear direction. Transformational leaders enhance their team members' motivation, morale, and performance by acting as role models, understanding their strengths and weaknesses, and employing the best personal and team development practices, such as optimizing tasks and improving performance efficiency (Folke et al., 2005).

2.5 Transformational Leadership and Learning

Transformational leadership positively and significantly impacts organizational learning potential and knowledge management among followers, providing strong evidence for the link between transformational leadership and organizational learning. Furthermore, an informed culture enhances the connection between transformational leadership and the effectiveness of information management processes (Yukl & Becker, 2006).

Numerous empirical studies have demonstrated a positive relationship between the behaviors of transformational leadership managers and their employees' performance and explored the processes that ultimately influence performance outcomes.

Camps and Rodriguez (2011) focused on this issue by analyzing the mediating roles of contextual attributes (organizational learning potential) and subjective attributes (capacity for employment) within the framework of transformational leadership and individual performance. Their research examined a sample of 795 employees from 75 university departments using a multi-layer path analysis with a two-level data structure. The empirical findings indicated several positive relationships:

- Between an employee's perception of their workplace's potential for organizational learning and their perceived capacity for employment.
- Between an employee's perception of their manager's transformational leadership and their capacity for employment.
- Between an employee's perceived capacity for organizational learning within a company and their performance.
- Between an employee's capacity for employment and their performance.

The study concluded that transformational leadership and individual performance had the most significant impact at the group level. While the capacity for employment was considered a particular qualification, at the group level, the influence of transformational leadership on performance was mediated by the organization's capacity for learning.

By emphasizing the importance of the link between organizational learning and transformational leadership, Mohamed and Otman (2021) assessed the critical role of leadership in today's rapidly changing and challenging business environment. Organizations and companies that invest in organizational learning become more informed, scholarly-oriented, and knowledge-based. These organizations maintain environments that promote knowledge exchange and experiential learning, characterized by positive elements such as collectivism and team spirit. With a deep awareness of the importance of learning for an organization's long-term success, transformational leaders can achieve this high level of performance. Leaders who recognize the enduring value of learning are better positioned to elevate their company's performance to new heights.

Research findings conclude that there is a significant relationship between transformational leadership, employee performance, and organizational learning culture. An organizational learning culture significantly relates to employee performance and mediates between transformational leadership and employee outcomes.

2.6 Motivating Inspiration in Transformational Leadership

A leader's role in a transformational leadership style is to inspire and motivate the team toward significant achievements. This leadership approach is highly effective in achieving team goals and meeting expectations. Transformational leadership is defined within organizational culture as fostering a sense of ownership among employees and independence for high-level executives in their workplace (Cho & Dansereau, 2010).

Transformational leaders drive change through inspiration and motivation by creating a compelling vision for their followers. As exemplary role models, they set a standard for others to emulate, encouraging their followers to believe in their potential to exceed expectations. Transformational leaders inspire their teams by boosting followers' self-efficacy and instilling confidence in their ability to achieve beyond what they previously thought possible.

Rather than resorting to micromanagement, transformational leaders motivate their teams by empowering employees who are knowledgeable and competent in their roles. This approach fosters creativity, forward-thinking, and innovation in tackling challenges (Folke et al., 2005). A hallmark of transformational leadership is cultivating a sense of goal orientation in the workplace. By striving toward ambitious, breakthrough goals, employees are more motivated to engage deeply in their work.

Transformational leaders also focus on employee development, enhancing employees' ability to cope effectively in challenging work environments (Hardman, 2023).

Transformational leadership occurs when a leader inspires and encourages followers to optimize their performance and enhance their perceived capabilities to achieve better results. Through this leadership style and motivational inspiration, the outcomes achieved often exceed the expected limits (Cho & Dansereau, 2010).

2.7 The Meaning of Motivating in the Context of Transformational Leadership

Transformational leadership motivates positive changes in followers. In addition to being inspiring, energetic, and enthusiastic, transformational leaders show care and involvement in the process and focus on facilitating succession in each group member.

Transformational leaders motivate their employees and are exceptionally passionate about their work by clearly defining their group goals. They inspire, recharge, and energize other group members (Folke et al., 2005).

Transformational leaders focus on helping group members succeed, providing needed support, guidance, and inspiration for working harder, and maintaining their success and loyalty to other group members. Some of the most prominent goals of transformational leadership are encouraging growth, promoting loyalty, and instilling faith among group members (Yukle & Becker, 2006).

2.8 Transformational Leadership and Being Authentic

Being authentic means adapting behaviors that reflect an individual's values, inner needs, beliefs, and goals, all rooted in a high level of self-reflectiveness and self-awareness (Jyoti & Bhau, 2015). An authentic transformational leader plays a central role in driving positive organizational change, genuinely aiming to serve others, remaining self-aware, and guided by core values.

According to Northouse (2017), leaders can develop their authenticity and necessary skills over time, promoting organizational success by adhering to a moral path and demonstrating transparency and attentiveness toward their followers. Genuinely authentic leaders base their actions on morality and uphold core organizational values, even amid transformational change. Followers need assurance that their leader consistently exhibits ethical behavior and maintains integrity, reinforcing their core values in everyday actions.

As George (2003) stated, "Being authentic leaders requires them to find the true north and be aware of it. A single essential leader qualification is to be a real, authentic person in all aspects" (p. 12). This involves knowing who they are, where they are going, and how to advance by adhering to their life values, setting the pace, and communicating their transparent expectations—qualities that develop over time. Cooper and Schriesheim (2005) suggest that authentic leadership emphasizes personal involvement, which fosters authentic development, sharpens a leader's skills, and facilitates team growth. Avolio and Gardner (2005) note that "positive psychological skills such as self-confidence, optimism, hope, and resilience are personal resources of the authentic leader" (p. 322).

Authentic transformational leaders make effective decisions, choose the right actions, set a strong example, and excel beyond their peers. The actual test for an authentic transformational leader is maintaining core values during change.

Transparency fosters a culture of trust between authentic leaders and their employees during transformational change. Followers must feel that their leader's transparency is upheld throughout all workplace communications. Northouse (2017) claims relative transparency means being open and honest about one's true self. Trust is established when individuals openly share their core emotions, motives, and tendencies. Both positive and negative aspects among team members must be communicated honestly, reflecting open communication and a relationship built on trust and integrity.

Employees who understand their team members' roles and the organization's overarching goals are more likely to trust their employer. Conversely, employees are often more inclined to leave a job due to their relationship with their boss rather than the job itself. Aligning employees involves understanding the whole picture and each team member's function, which requires workplace transparency. Transparent leadership enables followers to understand the company's vision and contribute to achieving team goals. Solutions can be reached more quickly by being open about challenges and involving employees in problem-solving. A culture fostered by authentic leaders that values transparency promotes team involvement and generates better outcomes (Cooper & Schriesheim, 2005).

An effective leader encourages others and recognizes both personal and team achievements. Northouse (2016) emphasizes that "leaders and followers are inseparably connected throughout the process of change, and authentic transformative leadership is socially oriented and deals with the common good" (pp. 162-163).

In our fast-paced, ever-changing world, leadership styles and approaches must be flexible and adaptable to meet constant shifts. Leaders must frequently make significant decisions and navigate conflicting beliefs while alleviating stressful situations. Influential leaders take ownership in times of trouble and assume responsibility for their mistakes. An authentic leader demonstrates the appropriate behaviors needed to address challenges effectively.

As the most efficient path, authentic leadership inspires followers, especially during periods of change. By presenting a genuine version of themselves, leaders evoke loyalty among followers who desire leaders with a moral foundation, transparency, and responsiveness to their needs.

Chapter 3: Organizational Change

3.1 Organizational Change – Theoretical Perspective

Understanding why and how organizations change is a central question in management and related disciplines. Researchers have explored these questions through diverse conceptual frameworks, drawing from biology, child development, and physics. Theories on transformational change and resistance to change offer varied motivations for change, different methods of managing it, and distinct roles and interests for participants throughout the process. The following sections present various organizational approaches to change and resistance, emphasizing the processes and roles allocated to individuals and organizations.

Classical approaches to organizational change often reference "planned change." These approaches suggest that dissatisfaction with the current state—due to poor performance, low revenues, inferior product quality, or a shrinking customer base—propels an organization toward desired outcomes. Albrecht et al. (2018) describe this process as "survival anxiety," where leaders, aware that they cannot achieve their goals without transformation, experience anxiety that generates change. Such discontinuous transformation has a clear starting point and follows a discrete timeline. A well-known model depicting this transformation is Lewin's three-phase model (1948), consisting of "unfreezing," "changing," and "refreezing." Organizations can achieve the highest-level transformation by adhering to a structured approach involving initiating, implementing, and embedding change (Albrecht et al., 2018).

In these approaches, employees are often the focal point of change efforts. Even when such transformations are presented as "collaboration in the making," the process typically aims to increase involvement, often viewed as a tool to counter resistance (Beer, 2021) or secure valuable partners who can make significant contributions.

Traditional approaches, which view organizational change as a project planned at the highest levels and implemented throughout the organization, have been contrasted by alternative perspectives criticizing the "planned change" model.

Organizational changes can be classified based on various criteria, such as intensity, timing, impact on the nature of organization-environment interactions, and areas of change. Changes can also be categorized according to their implementation: expanding an organization's "product basket," discontinuing specific products or services, shifting core activities, or redirecting marketing efforts. Structural changes may involve reassigning activities and responsibilities within organizational subdivisions, altering managerial hierarchies, merging organizational units, and restructuring coordination mechanisms. Technological changes may include adopting new machinery, improving production processes, and enhancing work practices. Personnel changes may address employee attitudes, management styles, organizational development, workforce composition, communication, interpersonal relations, and shifts in organizational norms and values (cultural change). As a multi-compartment, interconnected system, a discrete change in one area can significantly impact others (Levi, 2008; Kotter, 2010).

Fox (1998) identifies seven types of changes that can affect employees:

1. **Physical Environment**: Changes in physical working conditions (e.g., relocating premises, altering workplace design).
2. **Work Conditions and Rewards**: Changes in working hours, salaries, bonuses, promotions, or pension terms.
3. **Occupational Changes**: Changes in job content, occupational fields, product range, and technology.
4. **Social Environment**: Forming new teams or restructuring under new management, clients, or suppliers.
5. **Structural and Political Changes**: Changes in organizational structure, internal networks, and power positions.
6. **Standards, Procedures, and Policies**: Introducing new procedures and setting different assessment or product standards.
7. **Values and Culture**: Establishing new organizational goals, ideologies, and visions.

Each of these changes can trigger a process within individuals, affecting them cognitively (perceptions, beliefs, thoughts, judgments), emotionally (feelings, moods, attitudes), or behaviorally (decisions, actions). For example, a cultural change might primarily impact cognitive and emotional dimensions, leading to subsequent behavioral changes, while social changes might directly affect emotional responses.

Albrecht et al. (2018) also support a "continuous change" approach, where change is not seen as a single event but as an ongoing process that evolves and accumulates over time. Organizational change can occur through continuous adjustments in work processes and social practices. As a recurring process, such change is embraced by the organization, reinforced over time, and can lead to significant organizational transformations (Levi, 2008). Bordia et al. (2004) suggest that social reality is in a state of continuous formation.

According to Beer (2021), efforts to "organize" or redefine a situation are attempts to impose order on an inherently fluid reality. Accumulating information, knowledge, and experience from various groups influences organizational processes. These learning and change processes often begin at the organizational periphery and eventually target its core (Albrecht et al., 2018). In this perspective, employees are active and significant contributors to change generation and initiation. Integration into the change process stems from their role as central organizational partners (Bordia et al., 2004).

Beer (2021) argues that organizations develop through prolonged learning processes in the "Learning Organization" approach. A core mechanism for facilitating this learning is dialogue, which can occur when people interact as equals, setting aside differences in status and function. Learning precedes change, which is neither imposed by a single entity nor forced but emerges from egalitarian dialogue. The ability to maintain such dialogue is critical in change management. However, the feasibility of sustaining "communication islands" where differences in status and function are set aside is essential for the organization's existence.

While learning and dialogue are essential, these approaches must be more accurate in the significance of power and control within organizations and their impact on interactions. They limit the potential for continuous change and the ability of individuals to participate actively in redesigning change processes.

3.2 Organizational Change of Members

In any approach to change, it is crucial to remember that organizational change signifies a transformation in the work environment for the individual members who comprise the organization. Organizational change requires individuals to adapt to numerous shifts; their roles may be redefined, their influence within the hierarchy may change, performance assessments may alter, and organizational values may shift. The literature provides evidence of many emotional responses to these changes (Levi, 2008). Furthermore, the more significant the changes for an individual employee, the greater their sense of ownership and emotional arousal (Albrecht et al., 2018). Supporting change is associated with positive emotions, while resisting change elicits negative emotions (Beer, 2021).

Fox's (1998) model outlines seven phases for instilling organizational change:

1. **Identifying and Assessing Weaknesses**: Understanding the weaknesses and diagnosing the primary problems the organization must address, including the external environment and its interactions with the organization.

2. **Goal Setting**: Developing tactical and strategic approaches to address the identified difficulties and weaknesses, redefining the organization's vision, and outlining a desired post-change state.
3. **Detailed Change Planning**: Establishing a change team, developing a coordinated plan, allocating necessary resources, and setting the groundwork for implementing and embedding change.
4. **Gaining Consensus**: Understanding sources of resistance and implementing strategies to overcome it.
5. **Executing the Change Plan**: Activating local initiatives to align with the overall strategy.
6. **Assessing Further Changes**: Monitoring the effects, repercussions, and results to reduce the gap between the change process and the original or newly developed goals.

Bordia et al. (2004) suggest that the change designation aims to evoke emotions such as pride and embarrassment in individuals. An organization can exercise control through this emotional arousal by guiding individuals toward "desired" thinking patterns.

The transition from a former state to a new one requires individuals to reassess their existing cognitive frameworks, regenerating new processes of interpretation, self-accommodation, and readjustment, ultimately creating new mental schemas (Albrecht et al., 2018). These changes impact managers (Bordia et al., 2018) and employees (e.g., Levi, 2008). The integrative changes that transform individuals have implications for various aspects, such as their self-image (Beer, 2021), intention to leave the workplace, and overall attitude toward it (Levi, 2008).

3.3 Organizational Change and Its Members' Identities

Many researchers have explored the relationship between managerial discourse and its effect on employees' core identities and emotional lives (Levi, 2008; Kotter, 2010). Recently, there has been growing interest in how organizational change processes affect the identities of their members. Research has begun to examine change as an intensive organizational process that entails a significant transformation. According to Beer (2021), a process's success depends on members' readiness to adapt to new "technologies of the self." However, this is still a developing viewpoint in organizational change research. Albrecht et al. (2018) profoundly address the challenges organizations face in change processes but do not fully explore the complexity of identity issues.

Beer (2021) claims that during periods of change, organizational discourse accumulates and forms a new framework for interpretation, helping members understand and interpret the organizational reality. The language used during change creates new analytical frameworks that promote certain behaviors and interpretations while diminishing others (Bordia et al., 2004). Levi (2009) argues that any attempt to influence behavior and interpretation is an effort to reshape identity, suggesting that initiating change creates a dialogue between the organization and its members shifting identities.

Research highlights the challenges organizations face in applying changes, suggesting that the complexity of transforming identities at both the organizational and individual levels contributes to the difficulties in embedding change (Bordia et al., 2004). This chapter aims to delve deeper into the complexity of identity issues in organizational change and explore their contribution to these challenges.

3.4 Organizational Members' Responses to Changing Efforts

The literature on embedding change in organizations primarily examines members' responses to change processes. These responses can be interpreted differently through the lens of identity issues. For example, Albrecht et al. (2018) describe resistance as reducing organizational control against management, identifying two types: formal (organized, overt, collective) and non-formal (spontaneous, less direct, including gossip, absenteeism, and cynicism).

Some scholars argue that significant changes can severely impact employees, leading to negative attitudes, diminished performance, and intentions to leave. Organizational change can evoke intense emotions such as anger, despair, and anxiety, even among initially supportive employees (Kotter, 2010). Levi (2008) suggests that such change can be seen as a system seeking equilibrium, with resistance serving as a response to restore the system to its former state.

A key source of negative attitudes is the loss of identification with one's workplace. Employees form attachments to their roles, colleagues, and job routines, disrupted during significant reorganization, creating anxiety and a sense of loss (Beer, 2021). Moreover, employees seek to participate actively in decision-making, desiring control during intense uncertainty. Open communication becomes paramount in these situations (Kotter, 2010).

3.5 Transformative Leadership Efficacy in Managing Organizational Changes

Transformative leaders significantly influence employee responses to organizational change. They foster employees' readiness and commitment to change and energize them to support change initiatives actively.

Faupel and Sub (2019) analyzed employees' work involvement and their perceived value of change as motivational mechanisms explaining transformational leadership's impact on employee behaviors during periods of organizational transformation. Their research revealed two key findings: work involvement and perceived value of change as mediating factors illuminating the leadership process. Transformative leadership enhances employees' engagement and the perceived attractiveness of change outcomes, increasing behaviors supportive of change.

By embodying transformational leadership behaviors, managers can positively impact employee well-being during organizational change, underscoring their roles as role models and change initiators. Through charismatic and vision-driven leadership, transformative leaders aim to effect meaningful organizational change, changing employees' concerns and developmental needs and reducing resistance to change (Fox, 1998).

A transformative leader can guide a company and its change processes more efficiently and successfully. This leadership style seeks to inspire and motivate employees, enabling them to initiate and sustain change and laying the groundwork for future organizational success. Transformative leaders use their strong vision and personal charisma to engage followers in pursuing shared goals (Kotter, 2010).

Chapter 4: Communication and Transformative Leadership

Communication is essential to organizational success, allowing leaders to align followers with the organization's purposes, goals, and needs. How messages are conveyed significantly impacts outcomes, making communication skills crucial for leaders. A Transformative leader must clearly articulate their messages and understand why effective communication should be central in enlisting and training their team.

To be effective, leaders' messages must be authentic, inspiring, and consistent, enabling followers to understand and adopt critical organizational changes and new initiatives. An essential skill for leaders is knowing what they want to communicate, to whom, how they wish to convey it, and the duration of the communication process. Leaders can establish an agenda that saves time and resources by delivering precise messages. Time is valuable; a leader's message must be concise and accurate to ensure it is heard and prevent confusion or misinterpretation in the future.

4.1 The Role of Communication in Transformative Leadership

The foundation of my innovative model is the assumption that a transformational leader manages through positive and frequent communication. Such a leader is not focused solely on self-promotion but on being considerate of others. Transformational leaders share their vision with their team members, involving them in shaping and coalescing this vision.

Implementing successful organizational projects often involves breaking down timeframes into smaller, manageable segments. Communication becomes a central component of project success by effectively engaging employees and enhancing outcomes. Managing people involves placing the right person in the correct position and facilitating proper time management. A leader must assure each employee they will receive the support needed to complete their work on time. This requires attentiveness to what is missing, asking the right questions about the feasibility of information and resources, and ensuring the right person is available at the right time to achieve project goals.

By building trust through efficient communication, transformative leaders can align employee efforts while inspiring confidence and security. Effective communication involves using specific examples and details to clarify the leader's message. Thus, a communicative leader's discourse reflects a genuine desire to understand others, particularly their thoughts, emotions, and viewpoints.

Compassionate communication fosters empathy, enabling leaders to express care and concern for others. For instance, a team manager who uses compassionate communication when delivering bad news can guide their team through transformational change. This approach nurtures a secure, supportive environment that encourages team members to express themselves and be receptive to necessary adjustments, helping them overcome distress.

Using nonverbal cues, posing open-ended questions, and providing undisturbed opportunities for response can strengthen intimacy with colleagues, demonstrating their contributions are valued. Open and transparent communication can manage expectations, address fears, and alleviate resistance by providing necessary information, explaining the reasons for the change, and clarifying its impact.

4.2 Building Trust Through Transparent Communication

Maintaining communication throughout a transformation is crucial to establishing trust. Transparent communication demonstrates a leader's appreciation for employees' input and concerns and commitment to keeping employees informed. This approach fosters a sense of confidence and reliability, enhances employee involvement and collaboration, and increases their readiness to embrace change.

In summary, effective communication during transformation is essential for ensuring clarity, managing transformational efforts, and establishing trust among all stakeholders, ultimately contributing to the successful implementation of change initiatives.

Leaders should develop a comprehensive communication plan that outlines the central message, target audience, communication channels, and frequency to ensure a consistent and timely flow of information throughout the change process. Transparency regarding the reasons for the change, its anticipated effects, and the challenges, risks, and uncertainties involved is critical to establishing trust and reliability.

Different stakeholders may have varying levels of understanding and apprehension about change. Therefore, leaders must tailor their messages to meet audiences' needs and interests, ensuring that every group receives relevant and meaningful information. Leaders should be proficient in using various communication channels to effectively reach their diverse audiences, including holding meetings and selecting appropriate channels to ensure information is accessible to all intended recipients.

4.3 Repeating Key Messages and Seeking Feedback

Reinforcing and consistently repeating key messages throughout transformations is essential for clearly and reliably communicating the vision, goals, and progress to all stakeholders. Leaders must show empathy and understanding for their team members' fears and challenges during transformational change and actively communicate their support, providing the necessary resources to help people navigate these changes.

Timely and consistent communication is crucial for keeping stakeholders informed about the organization's progress, challenges, and next steps for change. Consistent updates help maintain involvement and reduce uncertainty. Influential leaders continually seek feedback on their communication efforts and adjust their approach accordingly. They ensure their messages are clear and aligned with the intended purpose by being open to suggestions and addressing gaps or misunderstandings.

4.4 Communication as a Tool for Organizational Alignment

Transformative leaders work to redesign the organization's ethical climate, ensuring alignment with its core values by maintaining consistent workplace communication. They excel at articulating the narrative behind vision-inspired change, engaging all followers by helping them see opportunities at both the individual and organizational levels, and encouraging them to strive for performance beyond expectations.

Effective communication enables leaders to build trust, establish a shared vision, and foster an environment conducive to change. By maintaining transparency, demonstrating empathy, and actively seeking feedback, transformative leaders can ensure a smoother transition during periods of change, ultimately leading to organizational success.

Chapter 5: SALIMA and WOCA Model: An Innovative Approach to Crisis Management

5.1 Abstract

In this research, I present an innovative model for crisis management grounded in the principles of Transformative Leadership. This applied model has been practically tested, and the thesis's conclusions and recommendations are analyzed based on the outcomes of this application. The models developed and tested in this research are SALIMA and WOCA.

5.2 SALIMA

The SALIMA model embodies the following key elements:

- **Strategy:** Effective management over a dynamic landscape characterized by broad foresight, visionary leadership, and continuous vigilance.
- **Adaptive:** Creativity, flexibility, optimism, joyfulness, and excitement in facing new challenges.
- **Learning:** An emphasis on attentiveness, ongoing education, and curiosity to foster growth and development.
- **Inspiration:** Self-confidence and a deep commitment to values, utilizing informal communication and leading by example.
- **Meaning:** Finding and conveying purpose and contributing beyond personal standards and self-interest.
- **Authentic:** Management that is empathetic, transparent, clear, and honest.

5.3 WOCA

The WOCA model posits that managers operate within different zones of managerial consciousness:

- **War:** A war-zone managerial consciousness based on a state of conflict characterized by a binary win-or-lose mindset.
- **Opportunity:** A managerial zone of consciousness that seeks opportunities, allowing opponents to present their victory narratives. This is the "golden mean," aiming for a win-win situation.
- **Comfort:** The comfort zone of managerial consciousness, marked by resistance to change and missed opportunities, often resulting in a lose-lose situation.

- **Apathy:** An indifferent zone of consciousness characterized by a lack of initiative and enthusiasm. This can also lead to a lose-lose situation.

The researcher developed this model, built upon extensive occupational experience and proven managerial and leadership abilities. It demonstrates how to mobilize the efforts of various employees and stakeholders to resolve complex organizational crises, which often arise from significant organizational transformations.

5.4 Methodology

This research utilized a 36-item SLQ (SALIMA Likert Questionnaire), where each statement corresponded to a behavioral trait associated with one of the segments of the SALIMA model. Respondents were given five possible answers for each statement, allowing them to rate their responses on a Likert scale.

A fundamental working assumption of the researcher was that each participant would have different levels of self-appraisal, with some participants being more self-critical than others. Therefore, the relative scoring for each segment was particularly significant. For instance, while one participant's total SLQ score might amount to 70, another could be 90 for the same statement, reflecting their self-assessments.

The critical finding from this approach is that the mean scores for each segment could be either below or above the averages for the questionnaire segments. This variance allows for more precise identification of managerial characteristic styles as manifested in the responses of specific interviewees.

To meet the requirements of this research, approximately 180 interviews were conducted.

5.5 Research Population

The research population comprised managers from educational, healthcare, and private organizations. The interviewees included school principals, managers of business organizations, and medical institutions.

The research findings suggest that managers who base their leadership on the SALIMA model demonstrate particular strengths in leading organizational transformations. These managers scored highly in strategic and inspirational capabilities and excelled in imparting a sense of meaningful value to their followers. However, another finding indicates that some participants assigned significantly less importance to statements related to authenticity and learning capabilities.

5.6 Conclusions

A manager who practices and embodies the characteristics of the SALIMA model can be considered consistently conscious of opportunities, effectively operating in the "opportunity zone" of blue oceans. Due to their "SALIMA-ian" managerial style, such managers will likely create a win-win reality that fosters harmony and mutual partnership. This organizational approach contributes to establishing decent, positive human relationships among all partners, resulting in a situation akin to the "golden mean."

In contrast, some managers may sustain a warlike consciousness, acting as if constantly prepared for conflict. These managers typically operate in the "war zones" of the "red ocean" universe, often resulting in either win-lose or lose-win scenarios. Similarly, comfort-seeking managers who refuse to step out of their comfort zones or dwell primarily in zones of apathy are more likely to lead their organizations toward lose-lose situations and eventual failure.

Transformational leaders who embody the characteristics of the SALIMA model can help subordinates achieve unimaginable performances and accomplishments, surpassing their previous expectations. This model illustrates how a leader's work patterns can "open the door" for innovation. On an individual level, such leaders can transform attitudes and assumptions, thereby fostering the creation of collective interests essential for cultural realignment.

5.7 Preface

This research presents an innovative model for crisis management based on the Transformative Leadership framework developed over many years of professional experience. Organizational crises, particularly those involving transformations, often accumulate into processes requiring controlled and rational management to guide an organization through a controlled transformation. Managing the various meanings and implications of such transformations is crucial to minimizing resistance from change-averse employees.

5.8 Rationale

This research's framework introduces an innovative Transformative Leadership model for managing crises that may arise during organizational transformations. The model will be practically tested, and conclusions and recommendations will be derived based on the research findings.

The rationale for this research thesis stems from the observation that, until the development of this model, most literature in the field focused on how organizational crises driven by transformations were managed. The existing literature emphasized variables such as leaders' behavioral and activity patterns rather than the underlying psychological motivations that form the foundation of overt leadership behaviors. This emphasis is surprising given the significant conceptual and methodological advancements in fields like self-psychology and developmental psychology over recent decades, highlighting leadership research's importance and relevance. Despite these developments, research on leadership has often focused on behavioral traits rather than consistently examining leaders' personality and developmental characteristics. Such research typically regards leadership behaviors as dependent variables with the most significant impact on subordinates' attitudes and conduct. Consequently, several empirically based models and well-tested concepts have been developed to explain the underlying characteristics, motivations, and processes that define the phenomenon of leadership.

5.9 The Research Hypothesis

The central hypothesis of this research is to examine the effectiveness of transformative leadership in managing organizational crises following transformations. This hypothesis will be evaluated through a model for organizational crisis management developed by the author of this thesis.

The model was developed with the perception that transformative leadership has a unique leadership language. It proposes that a leader can align followers' efforts by fostering a cohesive discourse. Central to this model is the concept that communication motivates followers. However, a leader must first inspire a behavioral change among followers to keep them engaged in generating change, as they recognize their roles and the benefits they can gain from the change.

Recognizing that people differ significantly, the challenge for a transformative leader is to know how to touch the hearts of followers—every one of them—despite cultural, social, and ideological differences. Hence, the importance of narrative in steering the transformative wheel among followers.

The language of this model distinguishes between a transformative leader and other managers, so I have created a glossary with specific terminology to be used within the model. These terms serve as tools for transformative managers until they become ingrained in the process and harmonize with organizational thinking, behavior, and everyday practices.

The model is based on six segments, each characterizing an effective transformative manager. Each segment provides a detailed examination of these characteristics, offering a unique dimensional interpretation of their relative significance within the model. The formulation of the model, with its six segments, promotes opportunities and win-win situations, which are central to the larger constructs of the SALIMA and WOCA (consciousness zone theory) models that I developed to provide new insights. It should be noted that after gaining extensive professional experience across various managerial domains, including municipal and governmental areas, I have successfully led numerous organizational transformations. Throughout my career, I have consistently embraced the challenge of entering organizations in crisis and guiding them from crisis to growth.

Chapter 6: The SALIMA and WOCA Model Explained

6.1 SALIMA

While the Bass model emphasizes vision and vigilance, the SALIMA model expands upon these concepts by incorporating additional meaningful components that address the interface between strategy and adaptation. A manager employing the SALIMA model may examine strategic goals with a fixed destination in mind; however, they must also recognize that data and circumstances can change constantly. Therefore, decision-making processes must remain flexible and responsive to ongoing changes.

The SALIMA model operates on the principle of a dynamic map, where strategic vision is combined with analytical skills, realism, resourcefulness, and creativity. These elements form the foundation of effective managerial decision-making. This principle inspired the development of the "WAZE model," which, like the GPS navigation software WAZE, maintains a fixed destination but requires continuous reassessment and adjustment to navigate roadblocks and choose alternative routes. Decisions must be made in real-time while analyzing various implications, always with the final destination in mind.

S – Strategy

In the SALIMA model, the vision must be meaningful and transparent and serve as a call to action. As part of the overarching narrative, the vision is crucial for motivating all participants to actively contribute to achieving transformation.

Watchfulness plays a vital role in the adaptation process. Rather than being disconnected from the vision, watchfulness is integral to its fulfillment. It involves understanding and producing insights that ensure the vision remains unchanged despite difficulties and changes while allowing for necessary adjustments. This concept is central to the Porch model, which revolves around maintaining a steadfast vision while adapting to evolving circumstances.

"Far-reaching seeing" involves looking through metaphorical binoculars rather than eyeglasses to maintain a long-term perspective parallel to tactical decision-making. This mode of thinking is essential for transformational leaders. A far-reaching perspective emphasizes the importance of establishing collaborative, relational systems for the long term, preventing a fixation on positions or starting points and instead focusing on initiating processes and aligning interests with strategic decisions.

A - Adaptation

- **Creative:** A transformative process can often involve crises, self-reflection, suspicions, and a loss of confidence. Therefore, developing new solutions must begin with a high degree of creativity. Creativity in this context is not solely dependent on the leader's ideas; it also involves the leader's ability to foster a creative process through collaboration with various stakeholders, such as through "round table" discussions.
- **Flexible:** Flexibility entails more than just the assumption that only a manager can provide information and solutions; it also implies a readiness to adapt, remain open to new solutions, and consider a wide range of alternatives. It is about being continually attentive to potential solutions and selecting the most appropriate ones, ensuring that a broad spectrum of possibilities is always considered.
- **Optimism:** In this model, optimism reflects a leader's confidence in their potential to achieve goals and successfully guide a transformational process. It also involves transmitting this optimism to their environment, fostering a positive atmosphere.
- **Joyful:** According to the model, joyfulness arises from engaging in meaningful work. Doing itself increases happiness and satisfaction within the organizational environment, among clients, and all those involved.
- **Enthusiasm:** The process generates a sense of joy and enthusiasm in facing challenges and whatever may come. Instead of conveying premonitions or a lack of confidence, managers can communicate their excitement about addressing challenges, including anticipated setbacks. This approach offers an opportunity to showcase the transformational leader's managerial and leadership skills while striving for success, self-fulfillment, and excellence.

L - Learning

- **Attentiveness:** Effective leaders are skilled in active listening and remaining attentive to opportunities that align with strategic goals and the realization of their vision. They maintain an open mind, understanding that attentiveness is crucial for empowering others and remembering why their vision is meaningful. This form of "transformational attentiveness" is cultivated by being unbiased, allowing the maximum amount of information to enter without judgment or preconceived notions.
- **Learning:** Learning is fundamental in this model, as it should be informative, constructive, and transformative. Leaders are encouraged to embody the proverb's wisdom, "I have more understanding than all my teachers" (Psalm

119:99), transcending barriers such as ego, gender, authority, and social status to learn without inhibition.

- **Curiosity:** As Albert Einstein suggested, if given 60 minutes to solve a problem, he would spend the first 55 minutes asking questions. The ability to ask questions and remain curious reflects a willingness to leave one's comfort zone and live in the "opportunity zone." This aligns with the "Blue Ocean Strategy," where leaders explore uncharted territories. An open-minded, curious leader is more likely to identify new opportunities, as illustrated by the saying, "A shy person cannot learn" (Pirkei Avot 2:5) and "If you never ask, you will never know."

I - Inspiration

- **Self-Confidence:** Inspirational leaders exude confidence in their path, the ability to drive change, and the capacity to overcome setbacks and challenges. They maintain their determination and keep their team motivated, ensuring everyone remains committed to the collective effort.
- **Commitment:** This involves a deep dedication to those who have supported and partnered with the leader, adhering to the foundational cornerstones of vision and values. This commitment is crucial when a leader serves as an inspiring figure.
- **Values:** During critical situations or crises, there may be a temptation to deviate from core values or to act manipulatively or ambiguously. A leader within this model is defined by their steadfast adherence to their values, which serve as a backbone throughout the transformational process. Upholding one's values earns respect and recognition for idealistic leadership.
- **Non-Formal Relationships:** A "SALIMA-ian" leader fosters personal, informal relationships that touch people's hearts. Rather than relying solely on formal authority, such leaders initiate relevant discussions, persuading their teams through ideological, human, and social means while remaining attentive to others' perspectives.
- **Setting an Example:** A transformative "SALIMA-ian" leader leads by example in all aspects—from arriving at work on time to demonstrating persistence, tenacity, and a commitment to values and people. This behavior makes the leader a role model for subordinates and other managers.

M – Meaningfulness

Meaningfulness is the ability to instill a sense of purpose in organizational transformations, promoting values that benefit a broad range of people. It involves creating a better reality and fostering collaborative efforts among all participants.

- **Contribution Beyond Itself:** A transformational process can generate significant outcomes that affect other areas, directly or indirectly. For example, promoting municipal leisure programs and revitalizing a town's cultural life can stimulate the local economy. Similarly, substantial investments in education can attract robust populations and enhance the city's profile.
- **Beyond Self-Interest:** Actions should have value and contribute beyond personal gain. The aim is not only for "me and myself" but to create value for others, contributing to a broader community impact.

A - Authentic

- **Empathy:** Leaders with high social and human capabilities show genuine care and are familiar with each person's needs, empowering and aligning team efforts. Instead of showing sympathy, a leader understands followers' needs and provides appropriate support. By doing so, leaders guide followers through transformational processes, illustrating how change can bring innovative solutions that benefit individuals and their environments.
- **Transparency:** To build trust within the team, leaders must maintain complete transparency, removing doubt or suspicion that hidden agendas drive the process. Transparency is essential for rallying people's efforts and gaining trust in leadership and communication.
- **Clarity:** Leaders must convey their vision and values to inspire belief in others. Clarity is a prerequisite for a leader's ability to mobilize and motivate; followers cannot see how change will benefit them or their future without it.
- **Frankness:** A leader's word is perceived as reliable and truthful, free of hidden agendas. Trustworthiness is essential for a team to follow, trust, and believe in the leader, particularly in times of uncertainty.

6.2 The WOCA Model

The WOCA model describes how managers operate within different "managerial consciousness" zones that can influence the initiation of change. By navigating through these zones, managers' behaviors are shaped by their consciousness, which ultimately dictates their approach to leadership. The model suggests that when managers remain attentive to opportunities, they can shift toward "Blue Ocean" strategies—unexplored market spaces—provided they embody the transformational qualities defined by the SALIMA model. This implies that only managers with an "Opportunity" (O-type) consciousness can create win-win situations.

- **War Zone — War Zone Consciousness:** This zone is characterized by a mindset focused on conflict and competition, where listening is limited only to oneself, and winning is perceived as the ultimate goal. Managers in this zone exhibit aggressive behaviors, believe they are always right, and display rigidity in their decision-making processes. This approach often leads to a win-lose situation, where one side triumphs at the expense of the other.
- **Opportunity Zone — Opportunity Zone Consciousness:** Managers in the opportunity zone are marked by their attentiveness to others and understanding of relationships' importance. They demonstrate foresight for the long term, consider multiple alternatives, and employ creativity and curiosity in their leadership. These managers are continuous learners, actively seeking opportunities and fostering environments that aim for win-win outcomes for all parties.
- **Comfort Zone—Comfort Zone Consciousness: This zone represents managers** reluctant to embrace new initiatives and feel threatened by change. They prefer to adhere to the status quo and avoid taking risks or showing initiative. This mindset leads to a lose-lose situation with no progress or positive outcome.
- **Apathy Zone — Apathy Zone Consciousness:** Managers in the apathy zone need more attentiveness, initiative, and enthusiasm. They may also experience depression or lack belief in the possibility of change. This mindset results in a lose-lose situation characterized by stagnation and a failure to move forward.

6.3 Discussion

This research has examined various leadership development programs, revealing their substantial contributions to increased revenues and positive organizational outcomes. As a result, many organizations are encouraged to invest in leadership development programs for their employees to gain a competitive market advantage. A prevailing concept in the leadership literature suggests that leadership is less about being an innate quality and more about self-evolvement, indicating that there are efficient developmental ways to nurture these leadership traits. Research in this area focuses on identifying the characteristics and factors that facilitate the successful development of individuals into leadership and management roles.

Reflecting on my work throughout my career and the model I developed, I have realized the usefulness and efficiency of a transformative leadership style in provoking and motivating subordinates toward meaningful work, excellence, and high-quality work patterns that align with organizational needs and goals. Among the many leadership styles, some may only benefit a single leader or produce short-term results.

However, transformative leadership inspires a longer-term perspective, creating sustainable organizational practices and a win-win approach that benefits leaders, their organizations, partners, and competitors.

For example, rather than focusing solely on tactics or short-term objectives, a transformational leader prioritizes understanding employee motivations, acknowledging individual differences, and aligning personal fulfillment with the company's long-term vision. Such leaders do not fear challenges or constructive criticism; they empower employees to share their ideas and positively critique new directives. By encouraging risk-taking, leaders help all team members contribute impartially to shared achievements. Instead of practicing rigid leadership, transformative leaders build trust among employees, guiding them toward success and enabling them to learn from failures, thereby preparing the organization for sudden changes, such as reorganizations, resizing, or resource limitations.

In transformational management, the process may involve activities that initially fail, requiring reflection and analysis to understand the errors, learn lessons, and make necessary corrections for eventual success. The mindset—"I am not the failure; the activity failed"—emphasizes learning, persistence, and focused efforts to solve failed processes. Authentic transformational leadership positively impacts followers, fostering moral identification that leads to positive decision-making and action. Transformational leadership can also positively influence the ethical climate and behavior within the group. As role models, leaders transcend self-interests, promoting trust and cooperation within the workplace. Authentic leaders are driven by their mission, uphold a shared vision, maintain transparency and honesty, and manage decision-making processes to guide their teams through crises and challenges.

By enabling others to act, leaders enhance their followers' sense of self-worth and the significance of their contributions. Authentic leaders function as social architects who clarify values, foster a positive culture, and design strategies to achieve desired outcomes. Flexibility and adaptability in leadership styles and approaches are essential in today's rapidly changing world. Leaders must frequently make critical decisions involving conflicting beliefs and heightened tensions. Influential leaders take ownership of problems and share responsibility for mistakes, demonstrating appropriate behavior, especially during challenging times.

It is essential to distinguish between transformational and transactional leadership styles, which often need clarification. Transactional leadership centers around fulfilling specific requirements by offering rewards and benefits, while transformational leadership emphasizes intellectual stimulation, ideological influence, motivation, and individual consideration. Transactional leaders may achieve short-term compliance by rewarding specific behaviors but do not encourage transformative change. In contrast, transformational leaders aim for comprehensive organizational transformation, addressing operational costs, productivity, quality assurance, growth opportunities, and other strategic goals.

Understanding and managing resistance to change is crucial for achieving positive outcomes, such as initiating successful organizational transformations. Embracing change is essential for adopting new concepts, taking risks, and adjusting to evolving circumstances. Developing employees' openness to change fosters self-fulfillment and creates inclusive and equitable workplaces. Organizational transformations must be managed with controls that consider their impact on individuals and the organizational environment.

My research aligns with Fox's model for managing organizational changes, which outlines seven phases for embedding changes within an organization. The first phase involves identifying organizational weaknesses and diagnosing critical problems, including analyzing the external environment and its interactions with the organization. The second phase, goal definition, focuses on tactical and strategic responses to the diagnosed challenges, creating a vision, and outlining a clear picture of the organization after the transformation. After defining the goals and visualizing the future, a detailed transformation plan is developed, including establishing a team and setting timetables, budgets, and concrete procedures.

The fourth phase emphasizes securing consent for change from all affected parties. During this phase, the organization must understand the core resistance to change and develop strategies to overcome it, demonstrating that change can be an opportunity. The fifth phase involves implementing the transformation program in alignment with local initiatives and overall goals. The final phase examines further changes needed to institutionalize the initial transformation, monitor effects, and make necessary adjustments to achieve original or new goals.

My experience leading organizational changes has shown that resistance to change often stems from employees' misunderstandings of potential outcomes. This misunderstanding can create problems that require careful consideration. Employees may have many questions about the changes, but due to limited or inaccurate information, they often perceive transformation as imposing a new reality. In their cost-benefit analysis, they may view the latter as more likely, thus resisting change. This tendency is particularly prevalent when employees distrust the change facilitators and suspect ulterior motives.

To manage organizational change crises successfully, it is essential to understand employee responses to change processes. Based on the model I developed and extensive experience, I find two general categories of resistance to change. The first category views resistance from a social conflict perspective, where it arises as a response to organizational control, whether bureaucratic, technological, cultural, or normative. Resistance is seen as a struggle by subordinate groups to gain organizational power, reflecting a class struggle between management and employees. Here, resistance is a rational response to defend oneself, even if it lacks merit concerning the content of a specific change.

The second category attributes resistance to individuals' emotional and cognitive limitations. This approach draws from psychology, where "resistance" is viewed as an unconscious act that prevents a person from confronting the trustworthy source of their problems. It rests on three assumptions: resistance is an inherent trait, an uncontrollable action, and an obstacle to change commitment. The manager's role is to uncover resistance and help the individual overcome it to facilitate change. However, addressing individual cognitive limitations during change processes is time-consuming and resource-intensive.

I also believe that changes affecting one's self or organizational identity can trigger anxiety, making it challenging to accept change and increasing the tendency to resist. A manager should closely examine employees' responses to change, particularly concerning their sense of self. An individual's reaction to change depends on how much it threatens their self-concept. The more aligned the change is with an individual's self-concept, the more likely they will support it. Conversely, if there is little alignment, resistance is more likely.

The two categories—social conflict and individual characteristics—are ideologically distinct, yet both provide insights into employee behavior during organizational change. These behaviors may not always stem from the specific content of the change but are often influenced by broader social or psychological contexts. Therefore, it is crucial to approach employee responses to change as opportunities for dialogue and co-creation rather than mere resistance.

Transformative leadership plays a vital role in this phase, using communication to align individual and organizational efforts toward a shared opportunity. The challenge lies in understanding and engaging employees with empathy, listening to their motives, beliefs, and aspirations, and inspiring them to embrace change.

Traditional views on organizational change emphasize management's authority and knowledge, with employees merely expected to comply. However, I propose viewing employee behavior during change as a "response" rather than "resistance." Employee responses provide valuable opportunities for dialogue and cooperation in achieving transformation. These responses often protect organizational interests and contribute to co-creating successful change initiatives.

In conclusion, transformative leadership fosters a dynamic, inclusive environment where employees feel heard, valued, and motivated to contribute to meaningful organizational change. By engaging employees constructively, leaders can navigate change more effectively, creating a more resilient and adaptable organization.

6.4 Conclusions

The model I have proposed identifies a "SALIMA-type" manager as one who both practices and embodies the characteristics of the SALIMA model. Such a manager is consistently alert to opportunities, navigating within the "blue oceans" opportunity zone. Due to their "SALAIMAnian" managerial style, they foster a win-win reality, cultivating harmony and mutual partnerships. This approach builds respectful, positive relationships among all stakeholders, creating a "golden mean" situation where mutual interests are aligned and sustained.

In contrast, some managers may maintain a warlike mindset, behaving like they are constantly seeking conflict. Such managers are often found in the "Red Oceans " war zones," where outcomes tend toward win-lose or lose-win scenarios. Similarly, comfort-seeking managers, who resist leaving their comfort zones or remain entrenched in apathy, can lead their organizations into a lose-lose reality, ultimately failing.

Transformational leaders who wield the SALIMA characteristics can guide their subordinates toward extraordinary performances and achievements that were previously unimaginable. This model demonstrates how leaders' practices can "open the door" to innovation. On an individual level, they can shift attitudes and challenge assumptions, creating the collective interests necessary for cultural adjustments within the organization.

For decades, research in this field has explored the challenges associated with change resistance. Unlike change aversion, which is not uncommon, overcoming resistance can enhance the success of organizational initiatives. Sources of change aversion are varied, including fear of the unknown, discomfort with the potential loss of control, and an automatic preference for the familiar over the unfamiliar. Despite advances in the literature on managing organizational change, resistance to change remains a persistent challenge, particularly in the absence of effective, change-oriented leadership.

Addressing change resistance early can lead to more positive and productive outcomes. Organizations can encourage early acceptance of change by fostering an open, empathetic, and considerate environment toward employees, thereby enhancing long-term efficiency and productivity. Successful change initiatives will likely lead to acceptance and acquisition, enabling organizations to remain competitive in an ever-evolving environment.

My research aimed to demonstrate that my managerial practices were rooted in a transformational leadership style. Transformational leadership can generate changes in followers' expectations and ambitions. Rather than conforming to existing norms, it redefines them, fostering a sense of commitment to shared goals. Transformational leadership can increase awareness among individuals and organizations, prompting them to be more earnest about their vision and more committed to shared values and ideals. This leadership style encourages people to align their behaviors with their beliefs, fostering a culture of collaboration and mutual support.

Consistent with my professional experience and the model I propose in this research, effective leadership requires managers to organize and construct learning experiences that align with the organizational vision and needs standards. Managers should engage learners through meaningful occupational tasks, provide clear direction, and restructure experiences to ensure an appropriate work environment that fosters motivation, satisfaction, and fulfillment. By doing so, managers can create a culture of continuous learning and improvement, which is crucial for achieving long-term organizational success.

6.5 Personal Reflection

One of the most prominent challenges managers face when leading an organizational change is dealing effectively with the resistance of organizational members. Resistance is often perceived as irrelevant, stemming from power struggles or employees' emotional and cognitive psychological characteristics. However, my approach departs from this predetermined conception. Instead, I see resistance as one of many potential realities. Another potential reality is to perceive the wide range of employee responses to change as a valuable source of information for both the organization and the transformation process. Preemptively labeling these responses as "resistance" can undermine the possibility of maintaining a productive dialogue between management and employees during organizational transformations. It also prevents the organization from benefiting from the knowledge and insights that employees may possess.

From a personal perspective, transformational leadership managers often lead by setting an example and becoming role models through their conduct in the workplace. By exhibiting authentic behavior, these leaders inspire employees to achieve high performance. Instead of manipulating employees into working harder, they inspire them through a commitment to trust, transparency, respect, and appreciation.

To initiate organizational change, it is crucial to challenge long-standing beliefs and the status quo by fostering innovation, creativity, critical thinking, and problem-solving. Transformative leaders should create a comfortable environment for employees to explore new ideas and opportunities, encouraging organizational innovation. The aim is to establish a growth-oriented environment that excites all participants about digital transformations and other significant organizational initiatives.

A transformative leader must help their team feel more connected and committed to the organization's vision. By aligning employees with the organization's mission, managers provide a meaningful goal that motivates them rather than using fear as a motivator. Organizational and employee growth capacity depends on how the culture and common language are managed. When transformational language promotes learning, curiosity, attentiveness, collaboration, commitment, values, persistence, and the pursuit of opportunities, it better equips the organization, its employees, and its leaders to identify and seize opportunities. This approach encourages moving beyond comfort zones to explore opportunity zones, where growth occurs in "blue oceans" rather than the competitive "red oceans."

6.6 Limitations

While there has been increased academic focus on leadership development programs, this research did not specifically examine the achievement levels of individuals who are naturally gifted in developing their leadership skills compared to those who may find such programs ineffective. Investigating this aspect could provide valuable insights and practical implications for this field of research.

6.7 Recommendations

To further explore transformational leadership, it is intriguing to consider its future directions. Although potential predictors for this leadership style have not been extensively researched, the literature suggests two possible areas for exploration. The first area is linked to the working environment of the leader, while the second focuses on identifying the personality traits of leaders.

The innovative model studied in this work provides empirical evidence and reinforces the idea that transformational leadership can produce positive organizational outcomes. From a research perspective, the literature offers avenues for further investigation into how subordinates perceive the impact of transformative leaders on various organizational outcomes. Additionally, more research is needed to understand the effects of transformative leadership on organizational climate. Such studies could compare the influence of transformative leadership on organizational climate with its role in managing crises driven by organizational change, examining whether these two functions can be complementary or contradictory.

From a practical standpoint, this literature review can help transformative leaders provide evidence for areas where their leadership style has proven most effective. The findings of this research may assist these leaders in honing their leadership skills to align with organizational goals and values, thereby maximizing their impact and achieving the highest level of outcomes for the organization.

This research presents a transformational leadership model in an organizational context, highlighting its significant influence on organizational and individual follower outcomes. The findings are linked to the impact of transformative leadership on organizational and follower outcomes, providing valuable insights for organizations in their leader screening processes. Organizations can consider these leadership qualities as future assets for growth and development.

This research proposes the SALIMA and WOCA models. It suggests that organizations should base their culture on a transformational language, specifically the SALIMA framework, which facilitates identifying growth opportunities at both personal and organizational levels. By developing a comprehensive terminology woven into a common language and implementing it within organizations, this research advocates for a mode of communication that aligns efforts to foster growth and collaboration.

Chapter 7: Speaking the SALIMA Leadership Language: The Terminology of SALIMA

Leadership is a language, and SALIMA is the language of leadership with terms that, when mastered and applied, create the ability to lead change and recognize opportunities according to the model.

Here are the 50 terms of the SALIMA leadership language:

1. **Vision as a Call to Action**

   The leader's vision is not merely a statement but a compelling call to action that energizes and unites all participants toward achieving transformational goals.

2. **Effective vs. Efficient Resource Management**

   Beyond merely managing inputs, an effective leader focuses on realizing the vision and the deeper meaning behind actions. Efficiency concerns what and why; effectiveness is managing resources to fulfill the vision.

3. **Conflict as the "Bubbling Pot"**

   Conflict is essential for driving change, challenging comfort zones, and motivating action. It generates value, sharpens alternatives, and refines processes. Leaders do not shy away from conflict but use it constructively to propel change.

4. **Living in the Opportunity Zone (WOCA)**

   A leader thrives in the "opportunity zone," constantly seeking ways to turn challenges into wins and creating a win-win scenario.

5. **Narrative: Telling a Story**

   Influential leaders communicate through storytelling, creating a compelling narrative that motivates and inspires.

6. **The Language of Leadership**

   Involves dialogue, engagement, and control over the flow of information to guide and direct the team towards shared goals. It emphasizes involvement, proficiency, and collaboration.

7. **The Attentive Leader**

   Provides open channels for communication, empowers employees by allowing their voices to be heard, and manages change through attentive listening.

8. **BATNA - Best Alternative to a Negotiated Agreement**

   Leaders must continually assess the best alternatives at any moment, understanding that "life is lived in alternatives."

9. **Empowering Context**

   Keeping the ultimate goal in mind, especially during difficult moments, helps the team cope with challenges and maintain motivation throughout the change process.

10. **The WIZ Model for Managing a Dynamic Vision**

    Like dynamic mapping, this model requires continuous assessment and adaptation, guiding actions while remaining focused on the ultimate vision.

11. **Living at the Intersection**

    Leaders thrive at the intersection of conflicting ideas, where opportunities are often hidden.

12. **Dynamic Mapping**

    Managing change through a constantly evolving plan, similar to a GPS that adjusts to new information without changing the destination.

13. **Future Orientation**

    Leaders maintain a forward-looking perspective, fostering hope and keeping their eyes on future horizons.

14.Clarity

A clear and compelling vision ensures all team members understand and align with the organization's goals.

15.Seizing Opportunities

Influential leaders are constantly looking for opportunities to advance the organization's objectives.

16.Blue Ocean vs. Red Ocean Strategies

Leaders must navigate between the "blue oceans" of uncontested market space and the "red oceans" of intense competition, seeking innovation and growth.

17.Building Coalitions

Leaders build strong networks and alliances to support and advance their vision.

18.Dancing on the Porch

This involves observing, learning, and gaining insights from an adaptive management perspective—balancing time on the "porch" watching with time "in the field" acting.

19.The Big Five Personality Traits

Openness, conscientiousness, extraversion, agreeableness, and emotional stability are vital traits that leaders cultivate for effective transformational leadership.

20.Living for What is Possible

Leaders operate in a world defined by what is possible rather than constrained by perceived limitations.

21.The Eternal Student

A commitment to continuous learning and understanding that true wisdom lies in recognizing how much remains unknown.

22.Constructive Learning

Learning is both constructive and contextual; it involves social activity, viewing failure as an opportunity for growth.

23.Growth from Collaboration

a. **Collaboration**: Bringing together diverse expertise to create something more significant than the sum of its parts.

b. **Coordination**: Avoid duplication by efficiently organizing tasks.

c. **Cooperation**: Uniting around a common task but not necessarily creating new knowledge.

24.Targeted Training for "Grit" Champions

Embracing the mindset: "I am not a failure; the action failed. What is missing will be done better."

25.XBC - Cross-Boundary Collaboration

Engaging beyond traditional boundaries to foster innovation and new approaches.

26.Optimism

Belief in the feasibility of realizing the vision, acting within a cosmos of actions rather than reasons.

27.The Shaping Leader

A leader who teaches, empowers, and cultivates others, nurturing the development of skills and talents.

28.Inspiration

Serving as a role model, source of motivation, and transformation for those around, thereby enhancing performance.

29.Responsibility

Unlike mere accountability, the leader takes proactive responsibility rather than waiting to be formally assigned it.

30.Trust

A belief in the leader's ability to realize the vision, their sincerity, and their confidence in achieving goals.

31.Commitment

Demonstrating passion and dedication to the work and the team's shared goals.

32.Cognitive Empathy

Understanding others' perspectives, asking questions, creating a welcoming environment, and gathering information are essential to better learning and care.

33.Transformation

Facilitating and driving change among team members, helping them see a vision for themselves and their future.

34.Transformative Learning

Learning through inspiration, sharing, and the experiences of others is transformative learning, which differs from mere knowledge accumulation.

35.Value Creation

Leaders create value using symbols rather than signals, guiding thoughtful decision-making processes that engage critical thinking.

36.Theory of Interpretation

Emphasizing the importance of the listener's perspective over the speaker's, understanding that messages are interpreted differently by different people.

37.Grit

A combination of passion, consistency, and perseverance that leads to success.

38.Purpose and Meaning

Essential motivators for action and persistence are shared through openness and collaboration.

39.Leadership Communication

It is not just about what is said but how it is said. Effective communication involves empathy, understanding, and authenticity.

40.Leadership as Conversation

Involves exchanging opinions, personal examples, mentorship, and authentic engagement.

41.Transformative Communication

Encourages a shift in perspective and behavior through open dialogue and shared experiences.

42.Beyond Personal Interest

Focusing on contributions that extend beyond personal gain and create broader impacts.

43.Contribution Beyond Self

Creating positive ripples that extend throughout the organization and beyond.

44.Providing Hope, Perspective, and Faith

Instilling a sense of optimism and excitement for the future.

45.Ensuring Happiness

Showing genuine excitement and belief in the team's goals and achievements.

46.A Leader of Values

Someone grounded in principles, characterized by integrity and steadfastness.

47. An Authentic Leader

Exhibiting integrity, loyalty, and commitment; someone who can be trusted and relied upon.

48. Adaptability

Motivating people to see change as an opportunity and to face its challenges head-on.

49. Honesty

Maintaining transparency in all dealings, ensuring trust and respect from followers.

50. Transparency

Communicating intentions and decisions to foster trust and commitment.

Chapter 8: The Path to the Model

Throughout my career, I have gathered many insights from each role I undertook, leading to developing a well-ordered theory. This theory outlines the methods and strategies for managing and leading a transformational process from crisis to growth. Below are the "milestones" that led me to develop this model:

It was during my graduate years at the Hebrew University, from 1985 to 1988, while studying general studies and history, that I explored three occupational paths: a journalist position at Yedioth Yerushalayim, a role as a parliamentary aide to Micha Harish, the then General Secretary of the Labor Party, and managing several Perach[1] projects at the university.

Perach is a national program that recruits students in exchange for scholarships to support academically challenged students. During the recruitment screening process, the Perach project manager identified my entrepreneurial and leadership qualities and allowed me to establish a new division of the Perach project from scratch. This role was an alternative to a position as a school program coordinator. As part of this position, I led various projects, guiding students through their activities and managing their work in different environments, including an institute for teenagers with autism, a program to help students prepare for matriculation exams, and the establishment of municipal youth councils in various neighborhoods across Jerusalem.

In managing these projects, I maintained personal contact with the students, supporting and empowering them while developing a deep understanding of their working environments. Through this experience, I gained valuable insights, including the importance of empathy, understanding people's functioning and behavioral patterns, recognizing their motives and priorities, and identifying meaningful and satisfying paths that can lead to a life-transforming lifestyle. I realized that life's meaning often lies in creating opportunities that motivate people to strive for self-fulfillment and achieve their dreams. In other words, people with a clear vision and supportive surroundings can build self-fulfillment with tenacity and self-assurance.

Reflecting on my journalistic career, I found it needed more meaningful engagement. I realized that reporting events that could shape or transform reality provided the satisfaction I sought. I desired a career that would allow me to create a better reality for people through transformation and enhancement. Retrospectively, I began to

[1] *Perach* is a national program for social impact. Also means a "flower".

understand leadership as the ability to guide people toward transformation. This insight ultimately led me to leave my journalistic position.

As a parliamentary aide to Micha Harish, I worked with him during a particularly turbulent period in Israeli politics, marked by the tension between two prominent leaders, the late Shimon Peres and the late Yitzhak Rabin, during Harish's tenure as Secretary General of the Labor Party. Harish played a bridging role between these two leaders. However, I did not feel that this political environment aligned with my aspirations, as I found it lacked authenticity and did not match my ambitions. Instead of pursuing power or social position to gain respect, I was more interested in engaging in meaningful work that would generate authentic feedback from people who valued my contributions. I found that my work in the public sphere was fulfilling only when it positively impacted people's quality of life. The professional aspects of the role appealed to me when they facilitated genuine and meaningful engagement, improved people's lives, and addressed their various needs.

Following this realization, my career path led me to a position as a community center director. I saw this as the right path for me. As a Perach project manager, I placed students in community centers (youth and sports centers) and integrated them into social activities. This experience opened up a new opportunity to become a neighborhood manager at the community center, a role that I found particularly compelling.

When applying for this position, I presented my philosophical beliefs, vision, heartfelt commitment to the neighborhood's residents, and dedication and motivation for taking on this role. I wanted the management to see me as a leader capable of driving meaningful transformations, someone who could heal the communal community center (which was then facing budget deficits and financial difficulties) and rebrand the neighborhood's image. The screening process for this managerial position was highly complex and time-consuming. It involved evaluating many highly qualified candidates, each with the required skills. Ultimately, I was selected after receiving the majority of votes from the management, confirming that I was the most suitable candidate.

This screening process allowed me to demonstrate to many people that I was the right person to take on the challenge. It also solidified several critical insights for me: the importance of building personal relationships, prioritizing the needs of others, and identifying how I could best assist them; being tenacious; understanding the critical power structures needed for the role; effectively handling resistance; understanding how my self-image was perceived both individually and collectively; and inspiring reliability and faith in others. These practices enabled me to create an environment of hope and confidence for those around me.

As an incumbent leader of the community center, I introduced a vision that reimagined the neighborhood as "the Savyon[2] of Jerusalem", recognizing its prime location and immense potential for development and renewal. One of the most pivotal decisions I made during my tenure was to transform "Gonenim"[3] into a local absorption area for new immigrants to Israel. This decision proved to be a catalyst for an organizational revolution, revealing numerous opportunities to realize my vision.

This decision's heart was transforming a collapsing, poorly managed, and visionless entity into a leading, innovative organization. This transformation initiated several additional processes, such as exploring the feasibility of recruiting further resources for immigrant absorption, securing new budgets to promote the vision, and winning various bids. It also included novel initiatives like developing community television, urban planning, and community-oriented policing. More importantly, this transformation demonstrated my ability to drive organizational change through successful, humane patterns of leadership and management.

In recognition of my successful efforts and the significant organizational revolution I had helped generate, the management of the community center Company awarded me a distinction prize. This award was particularly noteworthy because it was the first time such a distinction was given for such a short tenure;

The insights I consolidated during this period underscored the importance of establishing a clear, focused organizational vision that motivates and guides employees. I also developed a keen ability to identify and seize opportunities, such as the innovative initiative of creating a local absorption center for new immigrants[4]. My approach was characterized by empathy, a deep belief in the justice of my cause, rational thinking, optimism, and self-assurance. All these qualities were instrumental in overcoming the many complexities and challenges I faced during my tenure.

At 32, during this pivotal career phase, I was appointed to a mission for the Jewish Agency. Concurrently, the then Mayor of Jerusalem, Mr. Ehud Olmert, and his deputy, Yigal Amadi, who oversaw all the city's community centers, appointed me to manage the Pisgat Ze'ev Communal Administration. This neighborhood was also my home, giving me familiarity with complex problems.

---

[2] Savyon An affluent local community

[3] Gonenim, are a bunch of neighborhoods in the central-southern part of Jerusalem called also Katamons.

[4] During the 1990' the State of Israel saw waves of new immigration from the former USSR

Pisgat Ze'ev had undergone rapid population growth since its establishment, and by then, it had expanded to over 50,000 inhabitants. However, this swift growth created a mismatch between the residents' needs and the provision of services and infrastructure, resulting in strained relationships between the inhabitants and the municipality. As the largest neighborhood in Jerusalem, the Pisgat Ze'ev administration was responsible for managing businesses, representing residents, and providing a wide range of services, including leisure activities, sports, culture, and social services. It also had the full responsibility of managing the neighborhood's communal system. Despite its importance, the neighborhood had long needed adequate public infrastructure and institutions, which could not keep up with its rapid population growth. This shortfall led to significant tensions between the residents and the municipality, escalating to ongoing protests, public grievances, and crises.

These challenges also severely impacted the management and operations of the communal community center, plunging it into a deep organizational crisis marked by conflicts between management and employees. The community center Company's management issued a severe report recommending the dismissal of the current managerial team and the appointment of a new head of administration with the skills required to address the crisis. The goal was to rescue the community center and the entire neighborhood from the prevailing turmoil and transform it into a flourishing community while rebuilding productive working relationships between management, employees, and the Jerusalem municipality.

My appointment as the neighborhood manager directly resulted from my previous successes and professional experience in crisis management and organizational transformation. Recognized as a prominent leader skilled in these areas, I was seen as the right person to "heal" the neighborhood from its crisis. I was also perceived as capable of fostering the necessary collaboration between the neighborhood administration and the municipality to establish a professional, trust-based relationship. During my tenure, my abilities in transformational leadership were once again validated. Characteristics such as formulating a clear vision, inspiring employees to believe in it, and establishing integrative and trustworthy relationships among all partners were proven true.

I developed diverse services in this role, including community and social facilities for leisure, urban planning, and physical infrastructure. I initiated programs targeting seniors, new immigrants at the absorption center, youth, and special needs populations. I built a solid communal infrastructure supported by active volunteers and public management.

As I began my journey as the manager of the Pisgat Ze'ev Administration, I employed leadership strategies that allowed me to align the organization's rank and file, stabilize and reposition the organization, create collaborative relationships among employees, enhance team spirit, and guide the organization toward meaningful achievements.

During this period, I resolved many of the thorny issues that had plagued the neighborhood, leading to a remarkable turnaround in a relatively short time. As a result of this success, the community center management and educational staff decided to publish a manual titled "Model for Incumbent Managers into Office," which has since served as an academic and practical guide for managers in various organizations, especially those new to the community center system.

I framed the neighborhood with the superlative "Pisgat Ze'ev: The Lodestar of North Jerusalem" and led a new vision based on an integrative package of services for the northern neighborhoods. This vision included establishing new institutions such as a culture and sports center, a mall, an Israeli post office, and transportation infrastructure. Realizing this vision required significant municipal and governmental investments, which proved to be complex and challenging, highlighting the gap between vision and reality. This process required me to demonstrate a full range of leadership skills, particularly in crisis management, honed through various organizational transformations. My performance was closely observed by relevant municipal units, including the neighborhood principal and the administration employees involved in the process. I was evaluated based on my proven leadership skills, trust-based relationships, and adherence to my values.

Throughout this period, I successfully oversaw the establishment of several educational institutions, the construction of community center buildings and the mall, the improvement of sanitation arrangements, the enhancement of transportation access, and the allocation of green spaces. At the end of this growth process, my vision was effectively translated into practice through fruitful collaboration between the Jerusalem municipality and the various departments and employees of the Pisgat Ze'ev Administration. The success of these efforts set an example for implementing municipal services throughout all Jerusalem neighborhoods.

During the four years I served as the communal manager of the Pisgat Ze'ev Administration, my organization received numerous awards for excellence, particularly recognizing my managerial and leadership capabilities.

The insights I gained from this experience underscored the importance of leading with a clear vision, building trust-based relationships, and applying creative and "out-of-the-box" thinking. My ability to manage organizational transformations rationally and control while effectively handling resistance from change-averse individuals proved crucial to my success. By nurturing an environment of hope and confidence, I could align employees with organizational goals, leveraging practical skills, executive capabilities, and an aptitude for managing transformation-driven processes.

Alongside my fruitful doings, I enhanced the basis of my academic education when I participated in the Schwartz Program for the management of non-profit organizations at Hebrew University[5]. After graduating with distinction, I gained theoretical and practical leadership tools and continued training within various community center Company departments. This period gave me insights into the importance of individual learning, workplace optimism, creativity, mindfulness, empathy, self-empowerment, and team spirit.

After four years as the manager of the Pisgat Ze'ev Administration, several high-ranking executives from the Jerusalem Municipality, including Ranan Dinur (a significant source of inspiration for me), approached me to lead a transformative process at the Social and Youth Department. This department had been riddled with managerial and functional flaws, making a profound transformation necessary.

The transformation aimed to restructure the department into a central headquarters within the Jerusalem Municipality. The goal was to redefine its role in providing non-formal educational activities and shift all community buildings and clubs under the management of the community center Company. The objective was to reposition the department as a municipal hub, managing services through communal managers.

This change sparked a prolonged conflict with the community center Company, leading to a power struggle across the city. The department's workers' committee, staffed by long-standing grassroots managers, had come to view the department more as an aggressive entity rather than a professional one. Supported by the Jerusalem Municipality employees' committee, the entire personnel, including its leadership, vigorously resisted any proposals for organizational transformation.

It became clear that this transformation would be challenging for several reasons. One was that most department personnel had skills better suited for outreach work than for functioning as headquarters staff. They needed resource recruitment, training program development, and organizational oversight expertise.

---

[5] Schwartz Program – MA in Non-Profit and Community Organization Management. General information: The program imparts education and advanced training in managing non-profit institutions and community organizations in various fields.

Directing this transformation became a complicated management issue, eventually leading to a report by the Jerusalem Municipality, signed by Yigal Amadi, the then Chief Deputy. The report called for dismissing the senior leadership team and rebuilding a new organizational structure. This initiated lengthy negotiations between the municipal management and department officials, eventually reaching a consensus.

Following these negotiations, I was asked to lead the transformation. I underwent a complex decision-making process, navigating a municipal organization with a substantial workforce, political interests, and veteran employees with strong ties to the employees' committee. Many warned that initiating this transformation would likely fail, but I saw it as an opportunity to lead a meaningful process for the city and its residents.

I faced the reality of managing a multifaceted transformation. This involved engaging employees who feared and resisted change, including the employees' committee, financial personnel, legal advisors, external partners, and other municipal departments. Transformational change was rare in the local municipal environment and posed a perceived threat to different departments.

One of my key advantages was my ability to listen attentively to all employees' needs. I held personal meetings with each employee to understand their skills and preferences regarding their organizational roles. Some were offered new roles that better matched their capacities. I realized that the department's structure was ambiguous and lacked clear definitions of responsibilities. This ambiguity allowed me to motivate employees to take on roles that better suited their abilities, avoiding slow and cumbersome bureaucratic procedures.

Transforming the department into a municipal headquarters was a significant challenge. We successfully repositioned the department by harnessing the efforts of employees, management, and the employees' committee. We communicated a narrative that framed the transformation as an opportunity to elevate the department's collective image and grant employees greater authority to shape urban policy. This narrative instilled a sense of pride and prestige among employees, significantly boosting their motivation to work.

Aligned with the transformation management process at both department and municipal levels, I consolidated a vision of the department as a "municipal start-up" and an "entrepreneurial department." This vision leveraged the department's involvement with informal activities, using ambiguity in its roles as a strength for entrepreneurial ventures.

The vision emphasized the idea of an "urban start-up headquarters," with a staff capable of initiating various programs across various areas due to their close involvement with the community and non-formal activities. The department's operational branches and community managers could implement these programs.

Numerous initiatives began to take shape, and many projects were launched, positioning the department as a more robust and innovative entity within the Jerusalem Municipality. This innovation also allowed many employees to find new roles and generated promotion opportunities within the department.

My tenure at the Jerusalem Municipality was marked by several successful reforms and initiatives, including the establishment of new units such as:

- **The Youth Bureau**
- **Business Bureaus**
- **Populations with special needs**
- **Women's involvement and promotion**

Among the programs I developed, one groundbreaking initiative for adolescents with special needs earned the department a national prize for distinction. I was also personally awarded the Jerusalem TSAMID prize for my contributions to people with special needs.

The insights I gained during these years were numerous and meaningful. They highlighted the importance of forming coalitions, having a clear vision, striving for productivity, identifying opportunities, making controlled and rational decisions, acting from an authentic and transparent ideological foundation, supporting employees, and embracing the idea that failure can propel growth.

In each innovative project or procedure, I maintained a long-term, future-oriented approach guided by vision-inspired thinking. I focused on aligning employees' efforts and empowering them with empathy while forming coalitions and identifying opportunities. Every project provided employees with opportunities for renewal, prestige, partnership, coalition-building, and resource mobilization.

I completed an MBA in business administration during this period, fulfilling my commitment to continuous learning and development. My studies exposed me to innovative managerial theories, including the newly published Blue Ocean Strategy by W. Chan Kim and Renée Mauborgne (2004), which left a lasting impression on me. I frequently cited this book in speeches and used its principles to develop new strategies for identifying hidden and unexposed opportunities.

These insights enabled me to develop new programs within the department and expand its areas of activity. My success at the Jerusalem Municipality led to another job offer: to establish and head the newly created Culture, Social, Tourism, and Sports Administration. This role involved revitalizing the city and its leisure activities.

My strategy was to avoid conflict with veteran managers who became my subordinates. I chose a "blue ocean strategy," assuming these managers would eventually recognize the value of collaboration, personal fulfillment, and professional success. Otherwise, if they adhered strictly to formal management practices, they would find themselves in a "red ocean," where competition stifles innovation and productivity. My management style aimed to foster an environment that embraced all players, allowing personal expression, growth, renewal, and meaningful productivity.

The vision of "Jerusalem as a pilgrimage hub" and the transformation of the Jerusalem Culture and Leisure Administration turned the city into a vibrant center of cultural and tourism entrepreneurship, attracting interest from mayors across the country who sought to learn from our success.

However, a budgetary crisis soon emerged, hindering the city's securing grants from the Israeli Ministry of Finance. Severe budget cuts threatened to derail the realization of my vision and ongoing initiatives. During a critical budget meeting, I presented the narrative of Jerusalem's transformation as a success story that budget constraints should not hinder. I portrayed the activities of the Culture and Leisure Administration as crucial to implementing the city's vision. The meeting concluded successfully, with the municipality and its patrons committing to support our efforts.

In parallel with my work at the municipality, I completed a Master of Law (LLM) degree to enhance my education further and acquire theoretical and practical tools in the field of law. I am now a certified advocate.

Throughout these years, I also served on the boards of directors for various organizations across the city, aligning them fully with the realization of my vision:

- **The Yad LaBanim Organization**[6]
- **CEO in partnership with the community center Company of Jerusalem (now in liquidation)**
- **The Israel Festival NGO**
- **Ariel – an urban company for leisure time activities**
- **Eden – a company for developing the city center**

---

6 Yad LaBanim, an organization for commemorating IDF deceased soldiers and victims of terro

- **The Jerusalem Development Authority**
- **Bloomfield Science Museum**
- **Hora Jerusalem for folklore dancing development**

While working within the Jerusalem Municipality, I realized that although I had successfully addressed the city's challenges, I needed to fulfill my mission and reach my full potential. Driven by a passion for learning, an insatiable curiosity, and a desire for personal growth, I applied for the Wexner Foundation program. This program, which recently opened for the first time to chief executives, is part of the Kennedy School for Public Leadership at Harvard University.

Despite its short duration of just 1.5 months, this program became one of the most meaningful experiences of my professional life. It gave me groundbreaking insights that led me to rethink leadership's essence.

My Exposure to the Essence and Characteristics of Transformative Leadership

I went to Harvard with 40 more acquaintances from the highest Israeli public ranks. The reformative experience bore many ideas, new learning, and insights. This program was also created from thence on a professional network, and ever since, I have been stewarded by it. My exposure to the transformative world and various leadership models began at Harvard, including the current transformative I will represent.

On my second day there, I gained new insights into leadership as my colleagues and I took the Big Five Personality Traits self-test.

This model classifies five traits that leading managers usually boast about: openness (to new ideas), agreeableness (empathy), stable neuroticism, conscientiousness (planning), and extraversion (outwardly oriented, outgoing).

Similarly to my student-mate, I got my scores for the personal test, which allowed me to place myself in comparison with the mean scores of my class and parallel classes. This was an immensely intriguing outcome since my scores were above those of my class and other students, including all the tested traits. It reflected that except for one strength, the others matched the rest of the parameters. Synchronically, I realized that the toolbox I initially held throughout my career enabled me to lead many transformations. It was then that I realized what traits facilitate leaders in steering successfully a transformation, an insight which also shed light on what is needed for leading an organizational transformation: having the capacity to develop ideas, having both a creative and plan-oriented mind, being altogether emphatic, commanding, and obliging. For me, it portrayed exactly the affluent and enabling toolbox for the entire organizational transformations I had led across the many roles I played in neighborhood and municipal administrative directing missions.

However, I was not yet knowledgeable of the Five Traits Model underpinning, based on Bass' Model of Transformational Leadership, which would later underscore the model I developed.

The Harvard program enriched me with diversified insights and meaningful learning. I acquired the Principle of the Best Alternative to a Negotiated Agreement (BATNA) during the negotiation workshop. Practicing it with a classmate, he mirrored how I always seek appropriate solutions for both parties, namely a win-win opportunity for both.

The opportunity and win-win principles are at the heart of my model and a manager's consciousness analysis. A manager with an opportunity consciousness will always seek a win-win situation, letting your opponents give their triumph speeches. A manager with a discussion-aggressive consciousness will incur a win-loss situation. Practicing an apathy or comforting zone consciousness will result in a lose-lose situation.

My participation at the Wexner Foundation Executive Program exposed me to many models, where I conceptualized many cornerstone traits that intuitively I always acted and practiced according to them and exposed me to new ones as scaffolds for my developed model that I gained from the Harvard program and other learning processes during the Wexner Foundation training that served as food for thought and integrated well with my managerial concept. I found these models and many others taught at Harvard highly useful. Notwithstanding, the three most influential models I was exposed to also addressed management theory. Then, I started to develop my own XBC model (Cross-boundaries collaboration), adaptive management, and Mirpesset models, which we discussed at Harvard.

According to the model I built, Adaptive Management demands that a leader have traits such as adjusting during a transformation. To be adaptive means a condition for the ability to fuel a transformation for which orientation is needed. According to my model, traits like curiosity, learning, empathy, and vision are the basis for adaptive management and transformative leadership.

HaMirpesset (the Porch Model) mirrors a crisis management qualification, expressing an essential insight into the model I developed principally under the strategy. This principle claims that the capacity for dynamic decision-making in real-time and watchfulness is needed to generate organizational transformation. The Waze model was superimposed upon both principles, with the goal metaphor (the vision) as a road with many bumps and as a procedure for decision-making that can lead one to one's goal aided by an analytical consideration of alternatives.

XBC Cross-Boundaries Collaboration is a model that claims the importance of collaboration and recreating new knowledge against an ambiguous solution that calls for a learning process. This model taught me the importance of coalition formation among all stakeholders. Understand the importance of attentiveness and keep your management pattern ideological, reliable, and honest.

I encountered an imprint of significant milestones during the model I proposed therein. It later occurred to me during a transformative moment when I lectured at the Wingate Institution at an annual convention of sports managers. Opening my lecture with the following sentence: "... your challenge as managers and employees is to keep staying entirely at an opportunity area, which demands few things for doing ...". While these words were still reverberating in the convention hall, many scurries were heard in the audience when listeners were inquiring about the essence and meaning of these words. I said some meaningful words, an insight that opened everybody to new worlds of opportunities when I exemplified my words. The lecture ended when they requested to delve into a deeper discussion. It was then that it dawned on me that the meaning of "moving from comfort to opportunity zones" should serve as the hub of a transformative model that I developed later. I was enlightened by the idea that essentially stood at the core of my work, enabling me to generate many transformations.

While attending the Harvard course, a general election took place in Israel, and I decided that I wanted to be appointed to head a governmental office to elevate my passion to a national level. Indeed, I was appointed as the CEO of the Israel Culture and Sports Office, presiding over the ministry of Miri Regev.

During that issue, I brought many reforms to the world of culture and sports that had unrecognizably changed it. The transformation I headed rested on the same principles as those of the Harvard experience and had only nailed them further deeper. In sports, the vision was "the state is taking responsibility," and in culture, it was "cultural justice." Both bore endless reforms, all of which, due to the clarity of my vision, advocated for bending participants' efforts and taking opportunities. Two worth mentioning in the model transformative framework were the reform of the gambling market and the allocating responsibility to the sports and resources management from the hands of the Toto Gambling and Sports Company to the hands of the Culture and Sports Ministry. The Ministry of Finance, as a social statement, had asked me to suppress gambling; however, since money from Toto gambling has been catering to sports, I perceived it as a win-win opportunity for the Israeli Ministry of Finance and my Offices. In this move, I removed sports gambling money from its line in the Government Budget book. I put it into a line on sports budgeting that was issued instead to fulfill the sports vision of "A Country taking responsibility."

Another example of bending peoples' efforts and transformation was a ban set by Israeli Security Forces against the Hapoel Nahariya basketball team to join the European Cap final play against the Gaziantep team in Turkey. This ban elicited threats from the parts of the Turks and FIBA (THE International Basketball Federation). Also, it elicited much fear as to the status of Israel in the European League. I applied to the head of the Counter-Terrorism Bureau. All parties were presented at the discussion on my appeal, and I told them the story of the State of Israel. The narrative was that we must prevail everywhere; for this end, we must manage risks. I offered a win-win situation: we would lease an airplane, the minister would join us with her security guards, and we would return on that same day, and so it was. All partners have experienced transformation. The narrative was touching for everyone.

After five years of being incumbent in this office, I left for a chilling period. During that time, two of my kids participated in the Landmark program for self-development, which entailed learning and acquiring instructing tools for self- and personality-searching. The program motto was to help you understand "what is missing to make the difference," to help you be who you want to be, and to achieve self-fulfillment. I was intrigued mainly by the academic content of this program, so I chose to participate in the course as a guide for the program. Then, I was deeply exposed to its transformative content, and in this vein, I deepened my concepts on what transformative leadership must include: its characteristics, outcomes, and implications.

This learning widened my knowledge about the meaning of transformation and learning, about sharing that leads to transformation and authenticity. I then was passionate about writing a doctoral thesis in law about transformative legal bridging. With an eye on the full array of alternatives, I concluded that this subject had many issues that were neither connected nor involved in what I developed for the Transformative Leadership Model I developed. In light of my applied experience in crisis management and in leading a complex transformational change in the organization, I chose to scrutinize the model I had developed on transformative leadership in coping with organizational crises and in leading organizational transformational changes.

Chapter 9: Appendices

9.1 Methodology

This research adopts a qualitative methodology based on a humanistic approach to examine aspects of human behavior within its natural context. The study design is flexible, allowing for data collection through observations, open interviews, and text analysis. As a theoretical research project, the qualitative design is the primary research tool. The advantage of qualitative research lies in its capacity to perform causal analysis of events and draw conclusions within this context, avoiding using quantitative methods.

9.2 Research Tool

The primary research tool used in this study is the 36-item SLQ (SALIMA Leadership Questionnaire), which consists of items grouped into six segments corresponding to the SALIMA model's behavioral characteristics. Each segment includes five items that measure specific leadership traits.

The working assumption was that each participant would create their self-measurement scale, with varying degrees of self-criticism. The relative scoring of each segment is essential. For example, an SLQ total score of 70 for one participant versus 90 for another highlights how individual differences affect the interpretation of each segment. The relevant findings focus on specific segment means, determining whether they are above or below average for each questionnaire segment. This helps to identify the managerial characteristic style as manifested in each interview.

To achieve this, 180 interviews were conducted.

9.3 Research Population

The research population comprised managers from educational, health, and private organizations. Interviews were conducted in schools, business organizations, and medical institutions.

Sample SLQ Scoring:

- **Learning:** 70
- **Inspiring:** 80
- **Self-disciplined:** 95
- **Authentic:** 75
- **Total Scoring:** 482/6
- **Mean SLQ Score:** 80

9.4 Findings

The table below summarizes the scores for different leadership characteristics based on analyzing the research findings from the SALIMA-based leadership questionnaire.

Table 1: Summarization of Leadership SALIMA-Based Questionnaire

Characteristic	Items Assigned
Authentic	6, 9, 17, 20, 24, 30
Meaningfulness	5, 12, 16, 23, 29, 35
Inspiring	4, 8, 15, 19, 28, 34
Learning	3, 11, 14, 22, 27, 33
Adaptive	2, 7, 13, 18, 26, 32
Strategic	1, 10, 21, 25, 31, 36

Example of Strategic Scoring Calculation:

- **Item Scores:**
  - Item 1: 4 out of 5
  - Item 10: 3 out of 5
  - Item 21: 5 out of 5
  - Item 25: 4 out of 5
  - Item 31: 4 out of 5
  - Item 36: 3 out of 5
- **Total Score for Strategic Characteristic:**
  - Sum: 23 out of a possible 30, which equals 77%.

General SLQ Total Sum Calculation:

- **Scores for Each Characteristic:**
  - Strategic: 77
  - Adaptive: 85
  - Learning: 70
  - Inspiring: 80
  - Meaningfulness: 95
  - Authentic: 75
- **Total Sum:** 482
- **Mean SLQ Score:** 80

Chapter 10: Bibliography

Avolio, B. J., & Gardner, W. L. (2005). Authentic leadership development: Getting to the root of positive forms of leadership. *The Leadership Quarterly, 16*(3), 315–338.

Avolio, B. J., Bass, B. M., & Jung, D. I. (1999). Re-examining the components of transformational and transactional leadership using the Multifactor Leadership Questionnaire. *Journal of Occupational and Organizational Psychology, 72*(4), 441–462.

Bandura, A. (1977). Self-efficacy: Toward a unifying theory of behavioral change. *Psychological Review, 84*(2), 191–215.

Bass, B. M. (1985). *Leadership and performance beyond expectations*. Free Press.

Barthel, P., & Hess, T. (2020). Towards a characterization of digitalization projects in the context of organizational transformation. *Pacific Asia Journal of the Association for Information Systems, 12*(3), 31–56.

Bass, B. M., & Riggio, R. E. (2006). *Transformational leadership* (2nd ed.). Lawrence Erlbaum Associates.

Bass, B. M. (1990). From transactional to transformational leadership: Learning to share the vision. *Organizational Dynamics, 18*(3), 19–31.

Bass, B. M. (1997). Does the transactional–transformal leadership paradigm transcend organizational and national boundaries? *American Psychologist, 52*(2), 130–139.

Bass, B. M., & Avolio, B. J. (Eds.). (1994). *Improving organizational effectiveness through transformational leadership*. Sage Publications.

Beer, M. (2021). Reflections: Towards a normative and actionable theory of planned organizational change and development. *Journal of Change Management, 21*(1), 14–29.

Bordia, P., Hobman, E., Jones, E., Gallois, C., & Callan, V. J. (2004). Uncertainty during organizational change: Types, consequences, and management strategies. *Journal of Business and Psychology, 18*(4), 507–532.

Breevaart, K., & Zacher, H. (2019). Main and interactive effects of weekly transformational and laissez-faire leadership on followers' trust in the leader and leader effectiveness. *Journal of Occupational and Organizational Psychology, 92*(2), 384–409.

Buil, I., Martínez, E., & Matute, J. (2019). Transformational leadership and employee performance: The role of identification, engagement, and proactive personality. *International Journal of Hospitality Management, 77*, 64–75.

Burns, J. M. (1978). *Leadership*. Harper & Row.

Camps, J., & Rodríguez, H. (2011). Transformational leadership, learning, and employability: Effects on performance among faculty members. *Personnel Review, 40*(4), 423–442.

Cho, J., & Dansereau, F. (2010). Are transformational leaders fair? A multi-level study of transformational leadership, justice perceptions, and organizational citizenship behaviors. *The Leadership Quarterly, 21*(3), 409–421.

Cooper, C., Scandura, T. A., & Schriesheim, C. A. (2005). Looking forward but learning from our past: Potential challenges to developing authentic leadership theory and authentic leaders. *The Leadership Quarterly, 16*(3), 474–495.

Crede, M., Jong, J., & Harms, P. (2019). The generalisability of transformational leadership across cultures: A meta-analysis. *Journal of Managerial Psychology, 34*(3), 139–155.

El-Sayed, M. A., & El-Sayed, A. A. (2019). The impact of transformational leadership on front office satisfaction. *Perspectives in International Journal of Tourism and Hospitality Research, 2*(1), 1–14.

Faupel, S., & Sub, S. (2019). The effect of transformational leadership on employees during organizational change: An empirical analysis. *Journal of Change Management, 19*(3), 145–166.

Fayed, H., & Fathy, E. A. (2022). The impact of transformational leadership on front office employees' satisfaction and organizational commitment. *Pharos International Journal of Tourism and Hospitality, 1*(1), 49–63.

Folke, C., Hahn, T., Olsson, P., & Norberg, J. (2005). Adaptive governance of social-ecological systems. *Annual Review of Environment and Resources, 30*(1), 441–473.

Fox, (1998). *Psychology of resistance to change*. Bar-Ilan University.

Albrecht, S. L., Breidahl, E., & Marty, A. (2018). Organizational resources, organizational engagement climate, and employee engagement. *Career Development International, 23*(2), 67–85.

Fuller, L. (2021). Foundational leadership theory: An ethical leadership approach to developing positive employee work engagement. *Open Journal of Business and Management, 9*(5), 2136–2151.

Garzón-Lasso, F. A., Arenas-Arango, S. M., & Illera-Osorio, M. (2023). Is there a correlation between personality and leadership? A summary of the main theories. *Cuadernos Hispanoamericanos de Psicología, 22*(2), 1–17.

George, B. (2003). *Authentic leadership: Rediscovering the secrets to creating lasting value*. Jossey-Bass.

Hardman, J. C. (2023). Transformational leadership strategies in U.S. public universities. *Theses and Dissertations, 1318.*

Hater, J. J., & Bass, B. M. (1988). Superiors' evaluations and subordinates' perceptions of transformational and transactional leadership. *Journal of Applied Psychology, 73*(4), 695–702.

Heifetz, R., & Linsky, M. (2017). *Leadership on the line: Staying alive through the dangers of change* (New preface edition). Harvard Business Press.

Howell, J. M., & Avolio, B. J. (1993). Transformational leadership, transactional leadership, locus of control, and support for innovation: Key predictors of consolidated-business-unit performance. *Journal of Applied Psychology, 78*(6), 891–902.

Jiang, Y., & Chen, C. C. (2018). Integrating knowledge activities for team innovation: Effects of transformational leadership. *Journal of Management, 44*(5), 1819–1847.

Jyoti, J., & Bhau, S. (2015). Impact of transformational leadership on job performance: Mediating role of leader–member exchange and relational identification. *SAGE Open, 5*(4).

Judge, T. A., Bono, J. E., Ilies, R., & Gerhardt, M. W. (2002). Personality and leadership: A qualitative and quantitative review. *Journal of Applied Psychology, 87*(4), 765–780.

Kotter, J. (2010). *Change here and now*. Meter.

Kouzes, J. M., & Posner, B. Z. (2002). *The leadership challenge* (3rd ed.). Jossey-Bass.

Levi, P. (2008). *Management and leadership of change and innovation*. Ramon Publishing.

Lewin, K. (1948). *Resolving social conflicts: Selected papers on group dynamics*. Harper.

Li, Y., Castano, G., & Li, Y. (2018). Linking leadership styles to work engagement: The role of psychological capital among Chinese knowledge workers. *Chinese Management Studies, 12*(2), 433–452.

Lin, S., & Huang, Y. (2014). Examining teaching charisma and its relation to student engagement. *Cross-Cultural Communication, 6*(1), 1–8.

Manolika, M. (2023). The Big Five and beyond: Which personality traits predict movie and reading preferences? *Psychology of Popular Media, 12*(2), 197–206.

Mark, T., & Erude, S. U. (2023). Contingency theory: An assessment. *American Journal of Research in Business and Social Sciences, 3*(2), 1–12.

Mohamed, I. A. H., & Otman, N. M. M. (2021). Exploring the link between organizational learning and transformational leadership: A review. *Open Access Library Journal, 8*(1), 1–19.

Monehin, D., & Diers-Lawson, A. (2022). Pragmatic optimism, crisis leadership, and contingency theory: A view from the C-suite. *Public Relations Review, 48*(4), 102224.

Northouse, P. G. (2016). *Leadership: Theory and practice* (7th ed.). Sage Publications.

Oflatka, Y. (2015). *Foundations of educational administration: Leadership and management in the educational organization*. Pardes Publishing.

Oflatka, Y. (2018). *Emotions in teaching and school management: Collection of essays*. Institute of Inspectors.

Poetz, L., & Volmer, J. (2024). What does leadership do to the leader? Using a pattern-oriented approach to investigate the association between daily leadership profiles and daily leader well-being. *Journal of Business and Psychology*. Advance online publication.

Popper, M. (1994). *On managers as leaders*. Ramot Publishing.

Popper, M. (2007). *Formative leadership: A psychological view*. Ramot Publishing.

Popper, M. (2012). *Fact and fantasy about leadership*. Edward Elgar.

Popper, M., & Amit, K. (2009). Attachment and leader development via experiences. *The Leadership Quarterly, 20*(5), 749–763.

Popper, M., & Mayseless, O. (2007). The building blocks of leader development: A psychological conceptual framework. *Leadership & Organization Development Journal, 28*(7), 664–684.

Popper, M., Amit, K., Gal, R., Sinai, M., & Lisak, A. (2004). The capacity to lead: Major psychological differences between "leaders" and "non-leaders". *Military Psychology, 16*(4), 245–263.

Rick, A. R. (2018). Future-oriented identity: Necessary leader transformation through spiritual engagement. In J. Marques & S. Dhiman (Eds.), *Engaged leadership* (pp. 159–171). Springer.

Rotter, J. B. (1966). Generalized expectancies for internal versus external control of reinforcement. *Psychological Monographs: General and Applied, 80*(1), 1–28.

Shala, B., Prebreza, A., & Ramosaj, B. (2021). The contingency theory of management as a factor of acknowledging the leaders-managers of our time. *Open Access Library Journal, 8*(1), 1–20.

Smith, J. A., & Foti, R. J. (1998). A pattern approach to the study of leader emergence. *The Leadership Quarterly, 9*(2), 147–160.

Spielberger, C. D. (1972). *Anxiety: Current trends in theory and research: I.* Academic Press.

Stogdill, R. (1948). Personal factors associated with leadership: A survey of the literature. *Journal of Psychology, pp. 25*, 35–71.

Tao, Y. Q., Liu, X. P., Hou, W. X., Niu, H. Q., Wang, S. J., & Ma, Z. J. (2022). The mediating role of emotion regulation strategies in the relationship between Big Five personality traits and anxiety and depression among Chinese firefighters. *Frontiers in Psychology.*

Techo, V. P. (2021). Optimistic leadership for the 21st century and beyond. *The Journal of Values-Based Leadership, 14*(2), Article 8.

Xu, H., Jin, H., & Li, H. (2022). The relationship between leaders' long-term orientation and employees' innovative behaviors. *Creativity Research Journal.* Advance online publication.

Yukl, G. A., & Becker, W. S. (2006). Effective empowerment in organizations. *Organization Management Journal, 3*(3), 210–231.

www.ingramcontent.com/pod-product-compliance
Lightning Source LLC
LaVergne TN
LVHW022311200926
848481LV00004B/1293
9798892485753